BLACK-JEWISH
RELATIONS ON TRIAL

Black-Jewish
Relations on Trial

Leo Frank and Jim Conley
in the New South

Jeffrey Melnick

University Press of Mississippi
Jackson

www.upress.state.ms.us

Copyright © 2000 by University Press of Mississippi
All rights reserved
Manufactured in the United States of America

08 07 06 05 04 03 02 01 00   4 3 2 1

∞

Library of Congress Cataloging-in-Publication Data
Melnick, Jeffrey Paul.
Black-Jewish relations on trial : Leo Frank and Jim Conley in the new South /
Jeffrey Melnick.
p.   cm.
Includes bibliographical references and index.
ISBN 1-57806-286-1 (cloth : alk. paper) — ISBN 1-57806-287-X (pbk. : alk. paper)
1. Afro-Americans—Relations with Jews.   2. Frank, Leo, 1884–1915—Trials,
litigation, etc.   3. Phagan, Mary, d. 1913.   4. Jews—Southern States.
5. Jews—United States—History.   6. Afro-Americans—History.
7. United States—Ethnic relations.   I. Title.
E184.36.A34 M45   2000
364.15'23'09758231—dc21
00-036799

British Library Cataloging-in-Publication Data available

for Rachel Lee Rubin
— best friend and role model

CONTENTS

PREFACE

This book uses the example of the Leo Frank case to address the central question of Black-Jewish relations: how have African Americans and Jews been paired—as partners or competitors or some blend thereof—within the controlling American racial system of Black and white? With its pitting of an African American janitor, Jim Conley, against a Jewish factory manager, Leo Frank, in a contest to decide who was responsible for the murder of the young white woman Mary Phagan in 1913, the case is a perfect emblem for the erratic and dense history of Jews and African Americans: this history might be condensed in the image of a long and sturdy rope—some tie strong bonds with it, others get hanged.

Black-Jewish Relations on Trial attempts to call into question the dominant historical narrative of this relationship. My title is meant to suggest that the class of behaviors and utterances we call "Black-Jewish relations" might be best understood as coming to light most clearly in the medium of crisis. This book offers an investigation of the Leo Frank case of 1913–15, in which a Jewish man was tried for the murder of a young white woman who worked for him in an Atlanta factory. This case not only set Frank and Conley against each other but also produced (for a largely horrified public) a vision of New

South labor relations created by industrialization. It presents us with an opportunity to explore one specific "Black-Jewish relation" in all its complexity. The puzzling circumstances of the Frank case (if Frank didn't do it, then Conley must have) allow us to examine the racial and ethnic hierarchies of 1915.[1] Commentators have been puzzled for decades now that Frank was even *charged* with this crime, when Jim Conley was right there in the National Pencil Company factory looking suspicious (a bloody shirt, no alibi, and so on).

A new look at the case will call into question those narratives of a shared Black-Jewish history that are organized around the idea of a logically unfolding relationship: in my analysis of the Frank case "multiplicity" (of motivation, causation, and outcome) is introduced as a key term for explaining what goes on inside of the common spaces shared by Jews and African Americans. Frank and Conley were imagined by many to be in poisonously close contact with one another, apparently involved together in activities that marginalized both. Rather than the utopian possibilities so often presented by "Black-Jewish relations," the Frank case promoted the provocative notion that the connection of Frank and Conley functioned mostly to advance illicit (or at least unhealthy) social behaviors. With my analysis of the Leo Frank case I hope to demonstrate that this major event cannot be made to fit into any of the familiar renderings of "Black-Jewish relations"; in so doing I also want to forswear the (no doubt comforting) practice of narrating Black-Jewish relations as a simple and coherent set of events.

This criminal trial reminds us that important cultural discussions might begin in the courtroom, but they rarely end there. Trials are part of what James Scott calls "the public transcript"—a script that is endorsed (at least tacitly) by everyone involved, but which at best tells only a partial story about the workings of power (2). To understand fully the lasting cultural importance of the Frank case, we will have to look not only in the trial record but also in the "unofficial" record: the novels, plays, newspaper accounts, poems, web sites, and songs that have—in the eighty-five years since Leo Frank was lynched—attempted to set the record straight. As such, *Black-Jewish Relations on Trial* will treat the relationship of Jim Conley and Leo Frank as a story that has been a site of struggle for all these years. My own position on Frank's guilt or innocence is not relevant to the aims of this book: I am more interested in how the current generation of scholars has come to agree that Frank was innocent than I am in trying to present one more "whodunit" patchwork of the historical record. The aura of complete innocence that now surrounds Leo Frank has made it difficult to move beyond the exculpatory and into the analytical. The influential historian Deborah Dash Moore, for instance, writes about Frank in passing as someone framed "despite lack of evidence and obvious innocence" ("Separate Paths" 285); Leonard Dinnerstein, the historian of record on the Frank case for the last thirty years or so, has been quoted similarly as saying that "any open-minded person, given the evidence, would immediately say Frank couldn't have done it" (*Atlanta Journal and Constitution*, Feb. 12, 1986: A1). That Dinnerstein says Frank "couldn't have done it" (rather than the more defensible "didn't do it") gives a good idea of how difficult it has been in our own time to look critically at Frank's position in the matter of Mary Phagan's death.

Even if we accept that Frank had nothing to do with Mary Phagan's death, it is still necessary, for instance, to examine the ways Frank and his supporters used racist language to demean Conley and took refuge in what they understood to be the privilege of Jewish whiteness.[2] The "facts" that I will be interested in will largely consist of the dominant scripts in and about the case — in essence what people have written and said about the case; rarely will I weigh the plausibility of various claims made. Solving mysteries is a powerful and challenging project: the question I hope to answer here is not "who killed Mary Phagan?" but rather "why do so many people still care about the Leo Frank case?"

The last stages of preparing this book overlapped with my first two years at Babson College, and the timing could not have been better for me. Babson's Board of Research has generously supported this work at a number of different stages; Susan Chern, administrator of the board, and Michael Fetters, Babson's vice president of academic affairs, deserve special thanks for the work they do ensuring that Babson remains a congenial place to do research. I would also like to thank Dick Frost, my division's representative to the research board. My colleagues in the Division of History and Society have helped in many ways: I would especially like to thank Steve Collins and Jim

Hoopes—chairs, current and former—for doing so much to help me get my feet set. Peggy Carswell, Mary Driscoll, and Joan Walter also have my deep gratitude for their many kindnesses in helping me acclimate to Babson.

The research for this book could not have been completed without the expert guidance of librarians at the Georgia Department of Archives and History (especially Dale Couch), the Atlanta History Center, Brandeis University, and Babson College. I salute Kate Buckley at Babson for many acts of assistance, not least of which was tracking down a copy of *They Won't Forget* for me, after years of fruitless searching on my part. At the University Press of Mississippi I have been delighted to work with Seetha Srinivasan—all the good things I heard about her over the past years are true. Among other things, she arranged to have my manuscript critiqued by a reviewer who offered challenging and constructive suggestions. Anne Stascavage and Shane Gong, also at Mississippi, proved exceedingly helpful as I completed the manuscript. Donna Bouvier, at Harvard University Press, did not work on this book but provided me with a model a few years ago of how academic publishing works when it is at its best. I was also lucky to have Peter Hannan providing efficient and productive research assistance in the final stages of my research. Kevin Burke read the entire manuscript late in the game and made very useful editing suggestions.

Werner Sollors, Matthew Jacobson, and Judy Smith have all offered valuable advice, corrections, and encouragement along the way. Michael Rogin, whom I have yet to meet in person, has been remarkably supportive. David Maisel spent a hot summer many years ago translating Abraham Cahan's work on Leo Frank for me; along the way he also engaged me in many fruitful discussions about Black-Jewish relations more generally. Old friends Dan Miller and Mike Vorenberg read and commented helpfully on earlier versions of this work; Heather Hathaway, another graduate school friend, has also offered important academic help for years, as has Cheryl Greenberg—former colleague and dear friend. Heidi Feldman read portions of this book a long time ago and gave me advice on legal questions in the case; she has also been a valued friend for some twenty years. In ways less directly connected to this book (but more central to my daily life) I owe so much to my Cambridge neighbors, the librarians at the O'Neill Branch of the Cambridge Public Library, and the staff of Playspace.

This brings me to my merry band of Rubins. Jessie Lee, the shortest of them, finds countless ways to make me laugh; her resourcefulness and strength make me proud of her every day. Jacob fills me with awe: refusing to follow the dictates of what our culture says a boy can and can't be, Jacob blazes his own path—and by age ten has traveled farther than most grown men I know. Rachel Rubin—scholar, teacher, proud and loud feminist in a time of backlash, friend, co-parent, and partner—she puts it all together.

BLACK-JEWISH
RELATIONS ON TRIAL

Leo Frank, the Musical

Every retelling of the Frank case is bound to offer, to a greater or lesser degree, the same lesson... The outside world hates Jews and so Jews must cling to one another.

Samuel G. Freedman

In 1998 a musical about the Leo Frank case opened in New York City, with a story by Alfred Uhry (of *Driving Miss Daisy* fame) and music and lyrics by Jason Robert Brown, a relative unknown. When it came time to release the soundtrack for *Parade* in 1999, Brown was feeling flushed with success: in the notes to the compact disc, Brown recounts in a breathless rush some of the experiences he had while preparing the show. He remembers the "deafening applause" at the final dress rehearsal, and the gratitude he felt when Harold Prince, the legendary producer of the show, called him "the new Gershwin." Finally, he turns maudlin: "Two weeks before the opening, Alfred and I went to Leo Frank's grave in Brooklyn. Neither of us had been to see it the whole time we were writing together, and as we put two rocks on his simple gravestone, I looked down and thought, 'I hope we didn't let you down, Leo,' and as I thought it, Alfred said exactly the same thing" (*Parade* 9).

In 1999, to approach Leo Frank is to visit a shrine. For American Jews in particular, Leo Frank is a sort of talisman—a touchstone for Jews interested

3

in reminding themselves that they must, as Samuel G. Freedman notes, "cling to one another." Freedman's 1999 article on Frank culture in such a public forum is startling; few critics — Jewish or otherwise — have been willing to admit that invoking "the memory of antisemitism serves as a balm for intra-Jewish tension on such issues as intermarriage, conversion standards and the peace process in Israel. If American Jews still had to worry not only about lynch mobs but the exclusionary policies of law firms, country clubs, choice neighborhoods and Ivy League colleges, as they did for the first half of this century, then they wouldn't get so perversely sentimental about the Frank case." Frank's martyrdom has been gaining in power over the years. The weird-est of all visions of Frank, probably, was that wrought by Julie Ellis's 1980 romance novel *The Hampton Women*, in which a young woman, Elizabeth Hampton, becomes passionately involved with Frank's defense effort. In try-ing to capture the fervor of this young woman's commitment, Ellis basically turns Leo Frank into Sacco and Vanzetti. The internet has multiplied the op-portunities for sanctifying Frank: in the late 1990s it was easy to find resources on the Frank case (including various secondary school curriculum kits) put up by educational and civil rights organizations. Most of these web sites re-duce the case to a simple story of anti-Jewish prejudice.[1]

While the musical *Parade* stands as perhaps the fullest expression of pro-Frank sentiment, it is important to remember that there was a time when many people thought Frank to be guilty beyond a reasonable doubt. In fact, the first music written about Leo Frank took a much different position than that articulated by Jason Robert Brown and Alfred Uhry: when early country singer Fiddlin' John Carson sang three different songs about Frank, starting in public performance in 1913 and continuing on record in the 1920s, he sang of a demon who abused and killed poor Mary Phagan. In between Fiddlin' John's songs and Jason Robert Brown's songs came decades of competition over the meaning of Frank's legacy. But it is the bookends I want to begin with — what I'm calling *Leo Frank, The Musical*.

In this chapter I want to trace how Frank's story and image have been fought over — by Jewish Americans, African Americans, and other Ameri-cans — and what these fights have to tell us not only about Leo Frank but also about Black-Jewish relations (and race and sexuality more broadly) in American culture. Contests over the meaning of the Frank case and the Frank lynching have been fought out since 1915, when soon after Frank's lynching one Frank partisan wrote to Frank's widow, Lucille, to ask her permission to write a photoplay, which might help clear Frank's name. This woman claimed two major points in her favor: she knew David Belasco, the playwright and theater manager; and, as a Westerner, she was free from "prejudice of race or creed...unhampered by caste, unburdened by the formality of ancient family traditions which have been a curse to the South."[2] Even while Frank was alive many observers tried to rewrite the case along the lines of recognizable fictional genres and plots.

My intention is not to challenge the dearly held belief that Frank was innocent of Mary Phagan's murder. Instead, I want to explore why so many have set their sights on Frank and Jim Conley (but rarely Mary Phagan herself) as they make arguments about the relative status of Jews and African Americans in the United States. What has been largely forgotten in the "Frank stories" of the current generation is that Frank exerted enormous power over both Jim Conley and Mary Phagan in the National Pencil Company factory; this fact, and the discomfort it caused so many white southerners is, in large part, what lay behind Frank's arrest, conviction, and lynching. Instead, the late-model Leo Frank is a good boss, a good Jew, and a good husband (and in David Mamet's version, a philosopher too!). When the current generation "whitewashes" Frank, it erases the reality of his power in the National Pencil Company factory, and sidesteps the centrality of Black-Jewish relations to the case and to its legacies.

The story of the Leo Frank case has been told and retold. If Frank is not quite in the same league as Lizzie Borden, with her children's rhyme, countless true-crime books, and bed and breakfast (extra charge to stay in the actual room where her stepmother was killed!), this case has inspired the kind of cultural response matched by only a very few criminal trials. The case has received extensive coverage over the years, with historians, sociologists, advocacy groups, novelists, playwrights, and musicians all putting forth their own interpretations of it. The "rewriting" of the Frank case began before the trial was even over: according to some accounts, Fiddlin' John Carson was on the courthouse steps every day of the trial singing his ballad "Little Mary Phagan" to an appreciative audience.

Since then, the case has been revisited by a surprising range of people, including Fiddlin' John Carson himself (with two other songs about the case in the 1920s), two filmmakers in the 1930s, one "serious" novelist in the 1970s and one in the 1980s, a romance novelist in the 1980s, and two of America's most celebrated playwrights in the late 1990s. And this doesn't even account for a few other regional plays produced in the last quarter century. Even among academic historians, the case gets written in very different ways: in the two most recent scholarly accounts, the Leo Frank case has been studied by one as a treasure trove of information on gender and power in the Progressive Era South, and by another as a major anti-Semitic event (MacLean; Lindemann).

Major criminal trials often hold in them a remarkable amount of cultural energy. The very staginess of courtroom protocol invites participants and observers to create a good show out of what is very often the fairly mundane work of sorting out motive and evidence. Murder trials in particular offer up multiple satisfactions for spectators: invited to "get inside" the murderer's mind, viewers (at the trial in person, or following it in the media) are encouraged to dance with the devil. Come watch as the innocent maiden meets her fatal doom. There is, as many commentators have noticed, something at least faintly pornographic about recounting a murder in all its gory details, whether this retelling happens in the courtroom, in a novel, or on film. On some level, as historian Karen Halttunen has suggested, when men and women are asked to watch these "scenarios of pain," it is because they are meant to develop more sympathy for "the sufferings of others" (83). But it is clear too that murder narratives often titillate their consumers — especially when they emphasize the relationship of sex and violence.

The Frank case has been the subject of intense cultural scrutiny for much of the time since Mary Phagan was killed. Attention to the case has not been consistent nor has it taken predictable forms: Harold Prince's plans to stage a musical about Leo Frank were met with giggles more than once. Since the "facts" in the Leo Frank case were often obscure and always hotly contested during the trial and the appeals process, it is remarkable that so few of the retellings of the case have been concerned with solving the mystery of the pencil factory.

Unlike, say, Sacco and Vanzetti, or the Rosenbergs, Leo Frank's guilt or innocence is rarely debated these days. There is near unanimity around the idea that Frank was most certainly innocent of the crime of murdering Mary Phagan; it is something like unspeakable to suggest otherwise. Alan Dershowitz, for instance, begins his review of David Mamet's novel *The Old Religion* with the confident assertion that Jim Conley admitted to his lawyer that he had killed Mary Phagan himself; Conley's lawyer did make this claim, but no one ever got Conley to say such a thing in public — all other rumors to the contrary (128). In the last twenty years or so, the only people who have proclaimed their belief in Frank's guilt are Mary Phagan Kean, a grandniece of Mary Phagan, who wrote a book about the case; Tom Watson Brown, a grandson of the southern populist leader Tom Watson (who made a second career out of hating Frank); and Dr. Ed Fields, a chiropractor who was raised in Mary Phagan's hometown of Marietta, Georgia, and who is now the publisher of a white supremacist magazine which still carries on about Frank's deviltry.[3]

If I am going to make any sense out of the "Frank catalog" I will need first to present my own basic outline of the case and its legacies. In my version of the Frank case there are three main characters: Leo Frank, Jim Conley, and Tom Watson. The story I want to set up is one in which Frank and Conley are made to stand as representatives of what has gone wrong with the New South, a story that was largely scripted by Tom Watson. Watson was a populist leader who served in the Congress in the early 1890s, ran for vice president in 1896, and was elected senator in 1920. He also published two magazines (the *Jeffersonian* and *Watson's Magazine*) that carried his loud message: Frank was a lascivious capitalist come South to upset the delicate balance that southern whites and African Americans had achieved in the post-Civil War era.

Late at night on August 16, 1915, a group of "respectable" white Georgians broke into the State Prison Farm at Milledgeville and, meeting no resistance, abducted its most famous inmate, Leo Frank. By the following morning, Frank's lifeless body was hanging from a tree outside Marietta, the hometown and final resting place of the young woman he had allegedly killed (Dinnerstein 140).

After his controversial trial Frank received widespread publicity as his innocence was championed around the world; with his death Frank became a leg-
end and a touchstone.

Leo Frank was part owner and supervisor of the National Pencil Company
factory in Atlanta, and had been found guilty in 1913 of the murder of Mary
Phagan, a young white woman who worked for him for twelve cents an hour.
Although he was not formally charged with rape at this trial, intimations of
Frank's sexual perversion were essential to the prosecution's case and combined with familiar anti-Semitic images to make him a likely villain. What
was most unprecedented about the prosecution of Leo Frank was that its linch-
pin was Jim Conley, an African American janitor who also worked in the
factory. This represented the first capital case in postbellum southern history
in which a "white" defendant was condemned by the testimony of an African
American (Lewis, "Parallels" 547).

Mary Phagan was brutally murdered in the National Pencil Company factory on April 26, 1913. The day of the murder was Confederate Memorial Day,
and Frank was at the factory catching up on some paper work. Here is how
one historian of Georgia, writing in 1917, set the scene: "On this anniversary
of a Lost Cause, when the state was honoring its Confederate heroes with
memorial exercises, when the air was fragrant with garlands plucked by loyal
and loving hands to lay upon the graves of the dead, and when every one, in
response to an instinct of patriotism, was thinking in tenderness of the past,
there occurred in the heart of Atlanta a tragedy of the most revolting character" (Knight 1121). Frank himself took time out to write to his Uncle Moses
Frank to describe the parade he saw: "Today was 'yontiff' [holiday] here, and
the thin gray line of veterans, smaller each year, braved the rather chilly
weather to do honor to their fallen comrades" (qtd. in Connolly 36).

Phagan had not worked for a few days prior to this because a shipment of
metal casings for pencil erasers had not come in, and there was no work for
her. She came into Atlanta from an outlying suburb in order to pick up the pay
that was due her, planning to stay in town to watch the parade. Phagan's
family insisted that she worked at the pencil factory by choice, even after
her mother remarried and her stepfather requested that she stop (Kean 14).

Nonetheless, publicity surrounding the case highlighted the economic oppression of Phagan in the factory system.

Frank paid Phagan sometime between 12:00 and 12:30 and turned out to be the last person who would admit to seeing the young woman alive. Phagan's corpse was found at approximately 3:30 A.M. on Sunday by Newt Lee, an African American recently hired as night watchman for the factory. When the police arrived they discovered a body so covered with cinders that at first they could not ascertain whether or not it belonged to a white woman. Two notes, purportedly written by Phagan as she lay dying, were found by the body; both seemed to implicate Lee as the culprit. Suspicion attached to Lee briefly, but soon Leo Frank was fixed upon as the most attractive suspect. A few days after Mary Phagan's murder it became clear to Atlanta's police force that Newt Lee, who was being held in solitary confinement, was definitely not responsible for the crime. Further, the police were also starting to feel the pressure of a public clamoring for an appropriate villain to pay penance for this crime. The Atlanta police had been having a difficult time keeping up with increasing crime rates in the city — they had a number of unsolved murders on their hands at the time. Likewise, Solicitor-General Hugh Dorsey had recently "failed to convict two important accused murderers," and it is possible that his career hinged on getting a conviction in this case (Dinnerstein 19).

On the one hand, these conditions would suggest that a villain, any villain, would do: early suspicion of Newt Lee, with no material evidence against him, speaks clearly to this impulse. But very quickly, if we are to believe contemporary commentators, a special sort of blood lust developed; little Mary was a special victim (pure, innocent, one of "ours"), whose lost life demanded a special, outlandish miscreant as recompense. The pastor of Mary Phagan's church, in a contrite retrospective essay on the case, gives us insight into public sentiment in what has since become the most quoted evidence to support the idea that there was some kind of public call for an extraordinary villain: "My feelings, upon the arrest of the old negro watchman, were to the effect that this one old negro would be poor atonement for the life of this innocent girl. But, when on the next day, the police arrested a Jew, and a Yankee Jew at that, all of the inborn prejudice against Jews rose up in a feeling of satisfaction, that here would be a victim worthy to pay for the crime" (qtd. in Dinnerstein 33).

It is tempting to contemplate the workings of selective memory here: Pastor L. O. Bricker's testimony is an almost too perfect rendition of the argument that the Atlanta police went searching for an evildoer who would satisfy the public craving for an unusual type of blood. Many later students of the case have argued just this — that some kind of overwhelming public outcry put pressure on the law to come up with a suitable demon. Newt Lee, the night watchman, and Jim Conley, the janitor, both African Americans, simply would not do.

Let us consider who this "public" was. "Mary's people," as Albert Lindemann has aptly named them, have suffered ignominious description from generations of historians and journalists; in some respect I think this "silent majority" has, in a classic case of historical sleight-of-hand, become the true villain of the affair. Lindemann describes "Mary's people" as emotional, interested in a quick fix, and frankly unsophisticated:

> Ordinary people are not always capable of appropriately sifting through legal evidence, even when they have access to reliable information, which was hardly the case in the weeks immediately following the murder.... "Mary's people" did not need to engage in the intellectually taxing effort of sifting the accumulating mass of increasingly confused and contradictory evidence; they did not have to endure the psychologically difficult process of suspending judgment any longer. The "monster" had been caught, and what a satisfying conclusion! (249)

Steve Oney, in a 1985 article in *Esquire*, has taken this revisionist tendency to another level entirely. Describing a picture of the crowd surrounding Leo Frank's body after his lynching, Oney writes that most of the observers are "sunken-cheeked, nine-fingered rustics in bib overalls." One man in particular catches Oney's attention: he has a "lopsided jaw, crooked mouth, unfathomably stupid eyes — [he] conjures up the eerie sound of a banjo string tuned to the breaking point, a note of backwoods madness" (92).

The lynchers of Leo Frank certainly deserve to have calumny heaped upon their memory. But these poor rural people in the picture Oney is gazing at were deliberately excluded from the lynching party; at worst, they approved of the action and protected the identities of the lynchers. The killers of Leo

Frank were Marietta, Georgia's "best" citizens; Lucian Lamar Knight described the leader of the lynch mob as having "as reputable a name as you would ever hear" (1181–86). The demonization — or actually, celebration — of poor whites as responsible for lynchings committed by "best" citizens was not uncommon in the time of the Frank case; even as lower-class whites are forbidden from enjoying the pleasures of punishing the malefactor, the caste solidarity of all "normal" white people is reaffirmed by circulating the invented responsibility for the deed (Hall, *Revolt* 139, 303n24; Brundage 38; Berson 30). Of course this move also assures that the powerful white men responsible for the lynching do not have to fear prosecution.

But to continue to fasten blame on poor whites is to obscure the terms of the debate over Leo Frank's arrest, conviction, and lynching. No longer is this affair about contending status of African Americans and Jews in the South, no longer does it concern changing power relationships among numerous competing social groups; it now becomes a simple narrative of rural folks come to town to vent a little of their inbred savagery. One important point to make about the approach taken by Oney, Lindemann, and so many others is that they are, in effect, evoking a "third man theme" — popular among some creative artists too — in order to release the pressure that the Frank case put (and continues to put) on Black-Jewish relations. Drawing attention away from the complicated drama that pit Conley against Frank, and focusing mainly on Frank's martyrdom at the hands of a howling poor-white mob, these reports render the competition of African American and Jew in this case as an insignificant subplot. Blaming poor whites cannot erase the fact that Black-Jewish tension has long been a feature of the Frank case.

A starting point of the present study is that "Black-Jewish relations" is best understood as a Jewish story — a narrative of intergroup activity that speaks mainly to the desires of specific Jews. In this light it is important to understand how the persecution of Leo Frank has come to be a sacred text of American Jewish history, a key moment that revealed the vulnerability of Jews in America; stitching Leo Frank into this narrative has meant ignoring the "insides" of the case in order to squeeze it into a preshaped mold.

Once Newt Lee was cleared of any connection with Mary Phagan's death, Leo Frank loomed as the most realistic suspect. Complaints about his lascivious behavior were "discovered"; Frank was not only an employer of cheap labor and a Jew but he also had no supportable alibi at the time of the murder. But in the course of Jim Conley's affidavits to the police, it also became clear that Conley was a potential suspect. Conley seemed much more frightening than Lee; he had a prison record and a reputation for drunkenness, and, most telling, admitted to helping Frank dispose of Mary Phagan's body. Where Frank would never concede any guilt, Conley allowed himself to be implicated, at least as an accessory after the fact.

Why then was Conley not fixed as the prime (and only) suspect in the case? Here, as many have argued, seems to be where a real, if unarticulated, need for a "big" villain comes in. One observer of the trial and its aftermath argued for a police conspiracy to produce an appropriate criminal: "Conley was only a friendless negro, and to convict a mere negro of this crime, after the carnival of sensation and the mystery that had surrounded it, would make [the police] the butt of the community" (Connolly 50–51). A letter writer to Governor John Slaton made a similar point, with irony: "A mere roustabout, drunken, brutal, criminal negro would not satisfy this all permeating, absorbing, high class, soul stirring demand. . . . It would be too plain, too simple, too commonplace, lacking in mystery and sensation. Too much like things that had happened before to be the public solution of a 'great mystery.' "[4] Again, this writer reminds us that once the details of Mary Phagan's death became public, the "plot" of her murder had to be made to fit a satisfying pattern.

As a social drama, the Leo Frank case needed to provide its viewers with a recognizable form to organize its terrifying materials: as daily newspapers, people on the street, and Tom Watson began to piece it together, the form that seemed to suit the materials best was the Gothic. Mark Edmundson suggests that Gothic stories thrive "in a world where those in authority. . . are under suspicion" (20). Gothic stories are often rooted in horrifying structures (a decaying castle, for instance) that hold untold secrets within it. Frank's factory—his castle—stood in contemporary tellings of the case as the perfect emblem of horror. As far as most people could tell, the National Pencil Company factory was filled with gruesome occurrences; in the public mind, the usual factory architecture was transformed into a hellish scene of secret perversions and daily exhibits of Frank's demonic power.

Given the Gothic setup, it is not hard to see why Conley was let off the hook so easily. Whatever else he might have done at the National Pencil Company factory, Conley certainly did not run it. He did not fill balance sheets, or hand out pay, or look into changing rooms to make sure workers weren't taking "unofficial" breaks. Mary Phagan Kean, the grandniece of Mary Phagan, makes the usual case about Conley in her book on the affair: "It would have been easy to convict Jim Conley, a semi-literate, poor, friendless Negro with a chain gang record. Leo Frank, on the other hand, a white man with allegedly rich relatives, would be another story" (60). That position, which has become canonical in Frank studies, is misleading, because it ignores that the main work of the Leo Frank trial was to reckon with how power was to be organized in the industrial New South — especially in relation to the presence of African Americans and Jews. Mary Phagan — who always disappears too quickly from the set of Frank dramas — was an exploited young working woman. She was child labor. Frank was her employer. Frank was also Jim Conley's employer. Frank was probably not much worse of a supervisor than the average mill or factory boss in the 1910s. He also does not seem to have been much better than average. John Gantt, who was briefly a suspect in the case (and had been fired from the plant not long before the murder) called Frank the "president" of the factory: this reminds us that Frank was considered to be quite powerful by the people who worked for him (*Atlanta Constitution*, 29 Apr. 1913: 3). Again and again in the trial, in the appeals process, and in the press, Frank and Conley were weighed against each other, and weighed against the enormity of the horror visited upon Phagan. It would not necessarily have been "easy to convict Jim Conley" because the crisis that needed to be addressed did not have much to do with white southern fantasies of Black beast rapists or wild young African Americans at all. This trial had to do with Black-Jewish relations, and with the relations that African Americans and Jews were going to have with white southerners. That is why explicit comparisons needed to be made frequently between the competing scoundrels, Jim Conley and Leo Frank: in the course of the investigation and trial an implicit comparison was made, and Conley profited from the particular negative images that attached to him as an African American, while Frank suffered for those racial attributes assigned to him.

What was most important for Conley to do was to demonstrate that he could, essentially, take dictation for white southerners. One theory about the two murder notes found near Mary Phagan's body held that Conley did write them, but only as a stenographer for Frank. Conley himself suggested that it was Frank who taught him to write. What Conley needed to do before and during the trial was demonstrate that he was willing and able to follow the cues of the white southern men who were now running the show. For all the evidence presented against Frank at his original trial, it is clear that the key to his conviction was found in the testimony of Jim Conley. Without at this moment exploring too much of the detail of the case against Frank, let it suffice to say that Conley provided the Atlanta police and prosecutors with the missing piece that made their case: a motive. At some point in the investigation, Atlanta police learned that Conley could write. Additionally, his handwriting seemed to match that in the notes found by Mary Phagan's body. Faced with this incriminating evidence, Conley settled on an account that had him writing the notes as Frank dictated them, to cover for the crime Frank had already committed. Conley gave five separate affidavits to the police, a number which many thought *supported* Conley's veracity: according to Solicitor-General Hugh Dorsey, who led the prosecution in the case, "it was a constitutional habit of a negro to keep on lying until he finally lit on the truth" (qtd. in Connolly 51). On the witness stand Conley admitted that he often lied but told his listeners that it was easy to tell when he was doing so because he would hold his head at a particular angle (Golden 130).

In his fifth and final affidavit Conley came up with the key to Frank's conviction, the contention that Frank was a pervert. The precise evolution of Conley's affidavits will always remain a mystery; real possibilities include that the police provided him with his story, that he invented it on his own, or that—at least in some important particulars—he was telling the truth. Conley had every reason to lie, of course: even if he did not commit the crime of killing Mary Phagan himself, he may well have committed other crimes in the factory.

As Conley's final version of events put the matter, the country girl Mary Phagan died protecting her "virtue," thus making her an ideal heroine in a public narration that combined equal parts captivity narrative, Gothic horror, and anti-industrial melodrama. Commentators on this case consistently drew on literary conventions—not only Gothic ones but also captivity narratives, urban mysteries, and dialect pieces—to sort out the materials thrown up by this affair. When the great Jewish socialist journalist Abraham Cahan came South to meet Frank and study the details of the case, he finally became fed up with the purple prose surrounding it and referred to these narratives as sounding as if they had come out of a "junk novel" (513–14).

Although there was never any irrefutable proof that Phagan had been sexually assaulted, one speaker at a memorial service for her spoke of how she "gave up her young life rather than surrender that Christian attribute—the crown, glory and honor of true womanhood" (Dinnerstein 137; MacLean 936–38). According to Conley, Frank frequently entertained women in his office and had engaged with them sexually in a way that, when introduced at the trial, would make it clear that Frank, a Jew "Sodomite," was capable of any manner of wrongdoing (Woodward, *Tom Watson* 438). Perhaps no one was more interested in Frank's possible perversion than Tom Watson: again and again he explained to his magazine readers that only a Jew could have performed the disgusting behaviors that Mary Phagan's attacker supposedly (and there was never any convincing evidence of sexual assault) indulged in.

Frank's trial was tumultuous. The courtroom was packed with spectators, and the windows had to be kept open because of the excessive heat; some reports claim that cries of "Hang the Jew" could be heard in the courtroom (Golden 98–99). Forbidden by Georgia law from testifying on his own behalf, Frank did exercise the privilege of making an uncontested speech, taking many hours mostly to describe in detail the financial operations of the factory. After an initial guilty verdict and numerous unsuccessful appeals all the way up to the U.S. Supreme Court, Frank's death sentence was finally commuted by Governor John Slaton on July 21, 1915. In the two years between Frank's original trial and his commutation, Frank's friends and enemies became increasingly polarized. To his friends he was a Jewish martyr, made to pay the penalty for a crime committed by an African American man. To Frank's enemies, he was the picture of privilege: fears of Jewish money corrupting Georgia's judicial system (and later the federal government) intensified. While both Conley (as an admitted accomplice after the fact) and Frank languished in jail, African

Americans, Jews, and white Americans, were slugging it out over them. Less than a month after Governor Slaton, following much agonizing, commuted his sentence to life in prison, Frank's body would be hanging from a tree and Jim Conley wouldn't be much better off for it. The powerful white southerners who lynched Frank decided to put an exclamation point on the sentence that was handed down at Frank's trial: the Jewish man had to pay for the injuries of New South industrialism, not least of which was the way that "aliens" were coming to exert power over white women and African American men — a power that previously had been a special privilege enjoyed only by southern white men. White southern men had rigged a battle royale — we might as well call it "Black-Jewish relations" — and the fighters both lost.

The Black-Jewish tension at the heart of this trial was expressed in a number of the retellings of the trial in the "middle years" (the 1930s through the 1980s) of Leo Frank history. But bookending those more complex productions are the "Frank musicals" I have already mentioned briefly. What is most interesting about Fiddlin' John Carson on the one hand and the musical *Parade* on the other is how completely they preach to the converted. Carson (later joined by his daughter Rosa Lee) sang murder ballads that damned Leo Frank and beatified Mary Phagan to audiences of poor whites; Jason Robert Brown wrote songs for *Parade* that more or less ignore Phagan and not only clear Frank but render him lovable to a crowd of New York theatergoers. The songs of Carson and Brown are not meant to be challenging in either sound or sense: just as Carson's ballads grafted new (and not so new) lyrics onto familiar melodies, so does Jason Robert Brown craft songs that articulate safe conclusions in easily digestible fashion. *Parade*'s enthusiastic audiences heard in it plenty that they recognized — some Sondheim here, a little Andrew Lloyd Weber there, and maybe even a smidgen of *Show Boat*. In both cases the major themes and conclusions are givens: audiences applaud such performances because they confirm established beliefs, beliefs that are important to the audience members' perceptions of themselves. In the case of *Parade* it also seems worth mentioning that the usual musical stage rituals are all followed — including the one that has all the actors hold hands and take a bow together at the end, thus presenting a final image of reconciliation. The theatrical event ends with the audience applauding for the unified front presented by the actors.

Fiddlin' John Carson was the first major artist to try to reckon with the enormity of the social confusion created by the murder of Mary Phagan. Fiddlin' John's cultural significance should not be underestimated. Carson is a towering figure in the history of twentieth-century American popular music; he has been credited with having recorded the first commercial "country" song (Malone 75–77). To understand Carson's place in the history of the Leo Frank trial it is important to remember that he — like most "country" singers — was an urbanite by the time he recorded his music; it is not clear where Carson was born, but by the time of the Frank trial he was living in Cabbagetown, an area of Atlanta defined by its proximity to the Fulton Bag and Cotton Mill. Part of Carson's "work" was to explain to his audience — largely made up of people who had also migrated to Atlanta from their rural homes — what city life was all about. Rural to urban migration is perhaps the primary social fact underpinning the production of American popular music in the twentieth century, and it is certainly the central fact of Fiddlin' John Carson's career (Rubin).

With the trial of Leo Frank, Carson found a perfect symbol of the crisis of urbanization. Carson was not bringing the "news" to his audience: we have no precise numbers, but it is safe to say that a huge proportion of white Georgians believed Frank guilty during and immediately after the trial. Many of Carson's fans were "lintheads" — factory workers from the Fulton Bag and Cotton Mill. These workers enacted a work stoppage in October 1913 and went on strike in May 1914. As Carson recognized, poor white Georgians found in Frank a living representation of all that was making their lives miserable: he was a Yankee, a Jew, and perhaps worst of all, a boss. The voice of these disempowered workers, many of them first-generation city people, was Fiddlin' John Carson — himself a mill worker. Frank, on the other hand, not only was a boss but also had William J. Burns, a private detective, working for him. Burns was widely known and hated in Atlanta as a hired gun for the union-busting forces of Fulton Bag. Jacquelyn Dowd Hall explains that the labor strife at Fulton Bag had an exceedingly negative effect on Frank's case (Hall, "Private Eyes").

Carson began writing ballads about Frank and Phagan very soon after the murder; he may even have performed some of these songs at anticommutation meetings that were held in 1915. Tom Watson, the power behind the anti-Frank crusade inside of Georgia, was himself a fiddler, and it is tempting to think of Fiddlin' John as his musical representative (Malone 37). What remains valuable about Carson's murder ballads is that they remind us that it was more than plausible in 1913 to understand Frank as the villain in this case: while historical hindsight might exonerate Frank — his 1986 pardon from the State of Georgia which apologized for his lynching, but made no comment on his guilt or innocence, has led many to believe in his official innocence — Fiddlin' John Carson articulated a widely held belief that Frank had to be the murderer (and perhaps rapist) of Mary Phagan.

Fiddlin' John Carson understood immediately that Mary Phagan was a perfect hero for a murder ballad. When it came time to record his most famous song about the case, "Little Mary Phagan," John turned over the vocals to his daughter Rosa Lee (later known as Moonshine Kate) with the thought that her youthful, female voice would strike an even deeper chord with listeners. Country music historian Bill Malone has explained that women were often drawn to these "bloody ballads" because the very dramatic excitement of them provided an outlet for women "whose lives were blighted by deprivation and pain and loveless marriages" (25).

Carson used the murder ballad form because it was bound to resonate deeply with his audience: these topical songs, dating back at least to the sixteenth century, were often about men killing their lovers — frequently because the young woman's pregnancy was about to reveal the couple's sexual misdeeds. Fiddlin' John's two recorded songs about Mary Phagan (and one other he wrote, but never recorded, called "Dear Old Oak in Georgia" — about the tree from which Leo Frank was hanged) are fairly standard murder ballads. The first one ("Little Mary Phagan") even includes the traditional call to assembly "come all you good people" — though in this case it appears anomalously in the middle of the song (Wiggins 32–41). The story told by all of the songs is straightforward: Mary Phagan was a pure soul whose flame was put out by the evil and lecherous Leo Frank.

It is important to remember that performers like Fiddlin' John Carson were not in the business of making their songs out of wholly new materials. Quite to the contrary, a big part of Fiddlin' John Carson's job was to use familiar materials to carry new stories to his audience. In the case of "Little Mary Phagan" Carson basically adopted the tune of "Charles Guiteau" — sung in the voice of President James Garfield's assassin, and which was itself based on an earlier tune — and borrowed lyrics from all over the place. Perhaps most interestingly, two verses of "Little Mary Phagan" are taken more or less directly from a comic "Negro" dialect poem that dated back to the 1880s (Wiggins 36–37). During the time of the Frank trial Fiddlin' John lived on DeKalb Street in Atlanta, which was basically an extension of Decatur Street — the heart of what was known then as "Niggertown." In fact, one journalist of Fiddlin' John's era called Decatur Street "the melting pot of Dixie" (qtd. in Wiggins 24). But if Fiddlin' John's roots were what today we would call "multicultural," his social vision was decidedly monocultural.

This is why we need to go back and listen to Fiddlin' John and Rosa Lee Carson's "Little Mary Phagan" and Fiddlin' John's "The Grave of Little Mary Phagan" (also recorded in a different version in 1927 by Earl Johnson and His Clodhoppers as "Little Grave in Georgia"). Fiddlin' John Carson articulated a worldview that is almost completely absent from the contemporary historical record. His connection to, and understanding of, the murder of Mary Phagan has been overlooked in most accounts of the case for obvious reasons. First of all, he came down on the wrong side: clearing Jim Conley and blaming Leo Frank has become socially unacceptable in our own time. Moreover, Carson expresses his (and his people's) grief over the death of young Mary Phagan in language that is racist and anti-Semitic. In the three songs about Mary Phagan, Carson uses words like "nigger," phrases like "brutal Jew," and ideas about lynching (that it is the "work of justice," for instance) that are properly reviled in our time (Wiggins 41).

But what is worth paying attention to still is that Carson was using the occasion of Mary Phagan's death to contemplate the meanings of industrialism in the New South. While historians have long debated whether the populists were *particularly* anti-Semitic or not, it is clear from the rhetoric surrounding the Leo Frank case that it was a common move to blame the hurts of industrialization on alien Jews. In Fiddlin' John Carson's songs Leo Frank is evil because he is a Jew; an earlier version of "Little Mary Phagan," according to one account, rhymed "Leo Frank," with "New York bank" (Wiggins

32). For the many southerners who sent their children off to work, especially their girl children, the very fact of child labor was proof that something was deeply wrong with the current social order. To have one of their own killed while on an errand to collect her paltry pay was added insult. Leo Frank, as seen by the Atlanta police, by prosecuting attorney Hugh Dorsey, by demagogue politician and journalist Tom Watson, and by Fiddlin' John Carson, was to blame for everything that had gone wrong in the New South.

If pandering can be considered an artistic technique, then the makers of *Parade* have to be considered masters. *Parade's* strategy is to portray virtually all the characters as victims. The play opens with an iconic "victim"—a one-legged Confederate veteran of the Civil War—singing "The Old Red Hills of Home." Everyone in the play is suffering, not from anything so grimy and real as industrialization, but from a more mystical alienation, a sense of loneliness in the modern world. Alfred Uhry's banal insight is that while Leo Frank's conviction and lynching were based very much on Frank's inability to disappear into a new identity as a southerner, it turns out that southerners and Jews are inextricably linked on the symbolic level: after the Civil War, Uhry's script suggests, southerners became the Israelites of the United States, forced off the land they loved so dearly. Since at least early in the nineteenth century there has been a great deal of cultural energy expended on constructing an equation that brings together African Americans and Jews as fellow sufferers: from the African American adaptation of Old Testament stories for the spirituals through the countless twentieth-century attempts to draw connections between these two diasporic peoples in the United States, it has become a cultural commonplace to interpret Jews and African Americans as America's wanderers. The ugliness of Uhry's version derives from the way that he slyly substitutes all Southerners into the equation where African Americans usually go. Uhry talks all over the place about his dual identity as a Southerner and a Jew, but his major animus in this play is to create in Lucille Frank (herself Georgia-born) a character in whom southern and Jewish are complementary, not contradictory, identities. To do so, he has to—more or less—wipe African Americans off the board.

According to Uhry, all the people involved in staging *Parade* formed a "little Leo Frank family," and here he is not being completely metaphorical (qtd. in Simpson 22). Uhry's own great-uncle was Sigmund Montag, who owned the National Pencil Company factory and hired Frank to work there. Uhry remembers meeting Lucille Frank, who never remarried, when he was a boy growing up in Atlanta. Additionally, the chair of the Lincoln Center Theater, which sponsored the show, is Linda LeRoy Janklow, daughter of Mervyn LeRoy, the director who made *They Won't Forget* (1937), a film loosely based on the Frank case (Simpson 23). No smoking gun or conspiracy here, just a group of people interested in launching a show about Leo Frank that completely erases any notion that he might have been guilty of anything that might reasonably have made white southerners upset.

Uhry is right to suggest that the play makes everyone a victim, but it does so through generalization and hyperbole. Mary Phagan is mourned because she was so sweet: "she loved ridin' swings, / And she liked cotton candy" (*Parade* 16). The musical sidesteps the issue of Mary Phagan's emergent sexuality—and possible sexual exploitation—neatly and offensively. There is plenty of evidence in the trial record and in newspaper accounts from the time of the trial that Mary Phagan was the object of sexual interest inside and outside the factory: John Gantt reported that he found her beautiful and a young man named Arthur Mullinax told the *Atlanta Constitution* that he flirted with her during a church production of *Sleeping Beauty* that they both were in (28 Apr. 1913: 1).[5] But *Parade* ignores the charges of sexual harassment that were a cornerstone of the trial, except in one parody dance number where Frank sings "come up to my office" to various young women who work in the factory (*Parade* 19). This is not to say that *Parade* is a complete whitewash: in the musical, Phagan is presented as a flirt and Conley and Dorsey do hint at Frank's acts of sexual and labor exploitation. But *Parade*'s overall effect is to erase the complicated social relations that structured the case and its aftermath.

Jim Conley is rarely important to the action in *Parade*. Thankfully, the musical does not portray Conley as the bumbling fool he is in the 1986 television miniseries *The Murder of Mary Phagan*. As scripted by Larry McMurtry for television, Conley was a minstrel caricature, a killer too stupid to hide his lies. But *Parade*'s Jim Conley is full of righteous anger, aware that white folks would never care very much if a young Black woman had been killed. His two big numbers in the show ("A Rumblin' and a Rollin'" and "Feel the Rain

Fall") are — perhaps inspired by producer Harold Prince's recent success with a revival of *Show Boat* — basically "Ol' Man River" on steroids: voicing general protest against white racism, the songs do nothing to specify Conley's place in the racist labor system of the New South.

What is most noteworthy about *Parade* is that Jim Conley and Mary Phagan are merely footnotes to the main story. That central story is the love affair that bloomed between Leo and Lucille Frank while he was in jail: in Uhry's book Frank is rewritten as a lover. This accountant, whose face was studied during the trial for signs of perversion (which were usually found there in his "bulging" eyes and thick lips), becomes in *Parade* a man who is just searching for a way to make a real connection with his wife after years of being too busy with his work to take much notice of her. Very 90s. This leads to some bizarre plotting: the last scene before Frank's lynching has Leo and Lucille on a "picnic" at the state prison farm that ends with them making passionate love. (The audience cheers!) Immediately following this conjugal visit, Frank is kidnapped from prison; he seems most concerned at this moment to keep his genitals covered because he is still only wearing the shirt from the day before.

There are easy enough explanations for this focus on Leo Frank's genitals. As I will explain in chapter 3, Jim Conley testified at Frank's trial that Frank was "not built" like other men. For *Parade* to call attention to Frank's sexual ordinariness is a way to undercut earlier claims about his perversion. More troubling yet is David Mamet's suggestion that Frank was castrated. Unlike so many African American victims of lynching Frank was not mutilated after death. But visiting this horror upon him in historical reconstructions is a way to suggest that Frank did pose a "normal" genital threat to white southerners (Mamet 194). Even so, the distasteful masculinization of Frank is not the worst problem here. What is worse is the way that *Parade* (and Mamet too) takes as a given that Frank is the only character who truly matters in this unfolding social drama. Mary Phagan and Jim Conley are props — excuses to bring Leo and Lucille together. This makes for bad history and bad drama: *Parade's* point of view ends up looking every bit as provincial as that of Fiddlin' John Carson.

David Mamet's novel *The Old Religion* turns *Parade's* parochialism into a sharp ideological tool. It is not only "a fictional calamity based on a historical one," as one reviewer put it, but, as Alfred Kazin notes, it is also a violent piece of "Jewish jingoism" and "Jewish chauvinism" that could work to "sanctify every settler evicting every Palestinian from 'Judea and Samaria'" (Kazin 36–38; Giles 17).

In the history of "Frank stories" this is the one that makes it most clear how Frank can serve a variety of political aims — some quite nefarious. Mamet, for instance, turns Frank into a soul-searching Jewish intellectual who spends his time in prison pondering the mysteries of the universe and, more pointedly, the mysteries of being Jewish in America. Given that Frank's imprisonment coincided with the rise of Irving Berlin to national prominence it is more than eccentric to use the Frank case as an occasion to argue that Jews were making a big mistake in America by trying to assimilate. *The Old Religion* is the rarest of American Jewish artifacts — the antiassimilationist novel; Mamet has Frank meditate on the possibility that he is being persecuted mainly because he had the audacity to run a pencil factory in Atlanta and call it a "National" concern (49).

It would be tempting to dismiss the novel out of hand: it is terribly written, littered with faux-Faulknerisms — as when Mamet describes the judge and jury as upholding the "code, the amorphous code, the well-nigh or perhaps completely nonexistent code, to which they felt they had subscribed" (102). But it is worth pausing for at least a moment to consider how fully Mamet follows the basic design of *Leo Frank, The Musical* as first constructed by Fiddlin' John Carson and elaborated on by *Parade*. The use of cardboard stereotype and the division of the world into pure good and pure evil characterizes Mamet's Frank work just as it does Fiddlin' John's. Mamet's refusal to consider Jim Conley and Mary Phagan as three-dimensional human beings puts him on the same page as *Parade*.

In re-creating the final, fateful meeting between Frank and Phagan, as she comes to get her pay, Mamet has Frank at once *barely* notice Phagan (he is busy thinking deep thoughts about whether he should buy a paper clip holder for his office desk) *and* scope her out fully enough to decide that "he'd be hard pressed to have sex with her, as she smelled unclean" — meaning that she was menstruating (70, 79–80). Conley is not even granted enough subjectivity to have an odor. Mamet is too savvy to be blatantly racist: his "true-crime" story never sinks to the level of one written about the case in 1929, which refers to Jim Conley as "a slant-headed Ethiopian ape" (Sutherland). Whereas *Parade* could only really allow Conley and Phagan to exist in spheres separate from the one Frank existed in, Mamet instead writes them out of the picture.

In doing so, Mamet denies the social reality of New South Atlanta, a reality that brought Frank, Phagan, and Conley into daily contact. Creating a rarified life of the mind for Leo Frank, but no life at all for Conley and Phagan, Mamet writes an elaborate defense of his own turn toward Jewish orthodoxy. To be *properly* Jewish, according to Mamet, is to keep oneself apart and above smelly white women and stupid African Americans. In this, the novel reveals itself as a firm repudiation not just of Jewish assimilation but also of the New Left dream of Black-Jewish relations as part and parcel of the broad-based movements that included African American freedom struggles and women's liberation. Getting on Leo Frank's case is Mamet's way of saying no to alliance, no to integration. The ironies here are multiple and include the fact that it was Frank's lynching that inspired a number of powerful Jews (including the civil rights lawyer Louis Marshall) to dedicate themselves to working for African American civil rights (Lewis, "Parallels"). The sharpest irony, though, is that in the last quarter of the twentieth century, neo-Conservative Jews have often pointed to the separatist tendencies of Black Power leaders as one of the main factors in the destruction of the so-called "grand alliance" of African Americans and Jews. With *The Old Religion* David Mamet joins up spiritually with those white power activists who still use the Frank case as an excuse to advance racist aims. He also joins those advocates of a Frank pardon in the 1980s who pled Frank's case with a brand of rhetoric that was inspired, if not actually drafted, by the Jewish Defense League: "The Leo Frank decision shows how little the New South has changed. Once again bigotry and racism has raised its ugly head [sic]. History does not change. In the 1980s strong, proud and angry American Jews will not be lynched; rather Southern bigots will sway from trees" (qtd. in Freshman 160n20).

In between the extreme positions staked out by the various makers of *Leo Frank, The Musical* there have been some more measured attempts to reckon with the meanings of the Leo Frank case, most notably two 1930s movies and two novels published in the 1970s and 1980s. The two movies (Oscar Micheaux's *Murder in Harlem* and Mervyn LeRoy's *They Won't Forget*), along with Richard Kluger's 1977 novel *Members of the Tribe,* have the virtue of foregrounding the way that the National Pencil Company factory (traveling under various names in these works) forced interactions between all manner of people who might not have come in contact with each other had they not worked there. Ishmael Reed's 1986 novel, *Reckless Eyeballing,* is significant for the way it uses the Frank case as an example of how historical events get transposed onto the battleground of artistic representation.

By the time Ishmael Reed got around to shaking out the Leo Frank case its actual content had become virtually irrelevant. Although Reed certainly was interested in the details of the case (especially the charge that Frank had looked into the women's dressing room) what really seemed to matter to him was his own daring in rewriting this sacred text of Jewish history ("Liberal" 39). Noting the long tradition of appropriation of African American experience by Jews (he cites Jewish television producer Norman Lear in particular), Reed has complained that attempts by African Americans "to write about other major cultures is considered a case of 'Reckless Eyeballing.' What you lookin' at?" ("300 Years" 60–61). What Reed seems to have learned above all from the Frank case is that the manipulation of ethnic boundaries can cause real divisions, and usually serves ruling-class interests. Reed's response is to make the Leo Frank case his own text, even as he retains only the merest hint of its actual content.

Ishmael Reed's Leo Frank is twice removed from his real-life counterpart: in *Reckless Eyeballing* Frank exists only within a play at Mary Phegan [sic] College. Incorporating "Leo Frank" into his own text, Reed completes the process that began with Leo Frank's lynching, whereby Frank's specific experiences are effaced and thus prepared for inclusion in a chronicle of African American life. Reed uses "Leo Frank" to mediate some thorny questions about the ownership of artistic materials and so he invokes Frank not with any historical depth but only in the faintest iconographic outline. In Reed's hands "Leo Frank" comes to signify, finally, the contested ground of artistic production and representation on which African Americans and Jews have negotiated some of their most anxious and complex dramas. The historical Leo Frank had given way—in a process begun soon after his death—to "Leo Frank": inside of quotation marks, this rhetorical figure remains a pressing occasion for weighing the relative status and actual relationship of African Americans and Jews in the United States.

Like *Reckless Eyeballing*, the other three Frank texts are all intent on demonstrating that people rarely act from any single, pure identity: the director of a 1998 play called *The Lynching of Leo Frank* emphasized this point in an interview when he suggested that as an African American man approaching this material, he feels a connection to *both* Jim Conley and Leo Frank (Smith 1). The artistic works of Frank's "middle years" all turn Alfred Uhry's formula upside down: instead of suggesting that virtually everyone involved in the case is a *victim*, these texts suggest that actually almost everyone is a *villain*— from factory managers, to demagogic district attorneys, to flirty young women working in factories.

The two movies along with *Members of the Tribe* also admit—at least tacitly—that approaching the Frank case necessarily means reckoning with the status of Black-Jewish relations. All three try to undo the damage that the case did to Black-Jewish relations (deriving from the ultimate Frank-versus-Conley battle at its heart) by suggesting third-man solutions to the murder; this is muted in *They Won't Forget* and the novel it was based upon. *Murder in Harlem* explicitly pins the blame on Mary Phagan's boyfriend: following the details of the Frank case closely, this movie proposes a clever solution to the "he said/he said" conundrum of Frank versus Conley. In Micheaux's vision, the factory boss (now of the National Chemical Company) did force himself on the "little girl" who had come for her pay, did rough her up, and then did enlist an African American janitor to aid him in moving her body. But in Micheaux's movie the actual murder is committed by the young woman's white boyfriend, who has come to the factory with her. He sees the factory manager trying to kiss her, loses sight of her, and then finds her still-breathing body in a storeroom. Thinking that she is taunting him, the young man strangles the woman. The fascinating move Micheaux makes is to suggest that none of the principals in the action has enough information to be a trustworthy witness at the trial that follows.

They Won't Forget makes a "third-man" solution a real possibility as well. The real innovation of *They Won't Forget* (based on Ward Greene's novel *Death in the Deep South*) is to ignore Frank's Jewishness altogether and suggest that the case was the final battle of the Civil War. As the movie opens, the soundtrack plays a medley of "The Old Folks at Home," "Dixie," and "The Battle Hymn of the Republic," suggesting a cultural reunion of North and South (they are all Civil War-era songs) that the rest of the movie will then refute. This movie too follows the details of the case closely, even having the district attorney repeat Hugh Dorsey's original closing argument from the Frank trial, but with each reference to Jews taken out and replaced with "northern-ers." This film is the direct ancestor of Kluger's novel in that it populates the factory—here a business college for women—with a variety of villains, from an absurdly dictatorial southern white man running the school, to a Black janitor who spends his free time looking at naked pictures of white women, to Mary Phagan (here "Clay") herself, who is portrayed as a shameless hussy.

Kluger takes his cue from the two 1930s movies and goes much further. In his "third-man" rendition of the mystery of the pencil factory he daringly pins blame on a composite character he calls Joe Dettwiler, an old white man who has been sexually involved with Mary Phagan (Jean Dugan) ever since she confided in him that she has, on some level, been enjoying her stepfather's molestation of her. The real story here is that there is more than one story—and all of the stories are about the hypersexualized world of the factory and its environs. Rewriting nineteenth-century fears about the factory and second-ing Michel Foucault's argument about the repressive nature of sexual libera-tion under capitalism, Kluger creates a vicious world of exploitation in the factory: Frank and Conley's Black-Jewish relation is only one small part of a larger system of power relations in which each character dominates as many others as possible. Domination in this novel is almost always expressed in sex-ual terms.

Kluger's suggestion that Mary Phagan might have enjoyed being sexually abused is repugnant. But his convincing portrayal of the sexual life of the fac-tory works to reveal, finally, that the real "mystery" of the pencil factory was that it threw into question the most basic gender and sexual arrangements in the New South. Picking up on hints dropped by Ward Greene, Mervyn Leroy, and Oscar Micheaux, Kluger suggests in his novel that all the rumors were true—at least in part: there was a brothel operating in the basement of the factory, which Leo Frank knew about, and Frank was sexually involved with another factory worker. In this novel the sex partner is a stenographer, which seems to be at once a liberal borrowing from *They Won't Forget* (which opens with a room full of women business students learning shorthand) and also a bad joke—vintage 1977—about male bosses and the women who take dictation from them. (This joke is finally turned on its head by Dolly Parton's role in *9 to 5*.)

Above all, the novel supports the notion that sending young women off to do factory work exposed them to all sorts of dangers. Kluger is occasionally led astray in his earnest attempt to understand the inner world of Mary Phagan (as with the molestation issue), but his general point seems sound: young women working in the factories faced a multitude of sexual dangers that created a world in which "choice" became a virtually untenable concept. When Jean Dugan "chooses" to have sex with Joseph Dettwiler or Vernon Pike (based on John Gantt) it is impossible to feel that this is much of a triumph of free will. As Kluger notes in his afterword to the novel, it has never "been conclusively determined" who "really killed the Phagan girl" (468). One thing that his novel does conclusively show, however, is that new modalities of sexual interaction were a defining feature of modern factory life, and the relationship of Leo Frank, Jim Conley, and Mary Phagan has to be understood as an expression of that reality.

The "truest" versions of the Frank case are not those that stick most closely to the established facts of the case. Richard Kluger's novel sheds more light on the history of Leo Frank, Jim Conley, and Mary Phagan than any other artistic work inspired by the case precisely because it makes the factory itself the central character in this social drama. Fiddlin' John Carson and the Broadway team of Jason Robert Brown and Alfred Uhry (not to mention David Mamet) could not deliver any real *news* about the main players in the Frank case because they all tried to deliver fables devoid of context. Whether these artists turn Frank into a demon, a lover, or a philosopher, they all demonstrate a profound failure of nerve and imagination. Frank may well have been a demon, a (late-blooming) lover, and a philosopher—but he was given a starring role in the original production of what we have come to call "the Leo Frank case" because he was a boss. The Frank case derives its dramatic energy from the spectacular social instability that accompanied industrialization in the New South. For decades now—from the steps of the courthouse to the lights of Broadway—American artists have tried to alienate Frank from his labor context. What Richard Kluger helps us to see is that we can only begin to understand the fullest meanings of the Frank case if we stage it in a New South factory.

"THE NEGRO AND THE JEW WERE BOTH IN THIS"

Leo Frank and Jim Conley in Atlanta

It is impossible to offer a brief list of everything that was on trial during 1913 when Leo Frank sat in an Atlanta courtroom charged as Mary Phagan's killer. But it is clear that the ritual of the trial was meant to solve much larger mysteries than the one about Mary Phagan's demise. The main issues under debate in that courthouse all revolved around the question of whether industrialization and urbanization could be made to fit into the established system of racial and sexual power in Atlanta. Those enormous social questions were channeled by powerful white Atlantans through two main characters, Leo Frank and Jim Conley—alone and in their relationship to each other. The public reality of Frank and Conley, somehow linked in the world of the National Pencil Company factory (and as Richard Kluger suggests, also intimately connected to all manner of white Southern men and women), forced white Atlanta to reckon publicly with the realities of their changing city: the amalgamation that some white southerners had feared so desperately during the post-Civil War era was now becoming a reality—not necessarily in a sexual sense but certainly in the labor context.

"Black-Jewish relations," a phrase that in the last fifty years has operated for many people as a synonym for "Civil Rights Movement," had much more fearful connotations for many white Atlantans in the moment of the Frank case. The central purpose of this chapter, then, is to put Black-Jewish relations in places it doesn't normally appear: in the South, as a subset of Black-white relations, and in the domain of sexuality.

The expansion of southern industrialism that formed the heart of New South ideology in the post-Reconstruction era depended, as C. Vann Woodward and many others have explained, on female and child labor (Woodward, *Origins* 226). Mary Phagan herself, a few weeks shy of fourteen at her death, was continually characterized as embodying equal parts innocent waif and alluring woman. On the one hand, the murdered victim was dubbed "little Mary Phagan" in newspaper accounts, which for human interest value also noted that Phagan had recently played Sleeping Beauty in a children's church play; on the other hand, prurient interest was satisfied through the numerous descriptions — one provided by Phagan's mother on the witness stand — of how physically well-developed Phagan was for her age (Golden 100; Kean 17; MacLean 924–25).

This stark division in the portrayal of Phagan after her death was matched closely by images of the city of Atlanta in the Progressive Era. Louis Harlan captures Atlanta's split personality in his biography of Booker T. Washington: "Atlanta had always had a double image. One face was that of the trade center facing the dawn of a New South, standing at the junction of two major railroads. But its Union Terminal, gateway to the South, required black people to use a separate entrance into a separate waiting room. Bustling, commercial Atlanta never found a place for blacks except as subordinates and pariahs. One reason for this paradox was that Atlanta was not fully urban. Many of its whites were in rather than of the city, displaced country persons" (296).

The Gate City, burned out by Sherman and his troops during the Civil War, had been transformed into the prize city of New South ideology by the time of Mary Phagan's death. Henry W. Grady, managing editor of the *Atlanta Constitution* and number-one booster of regional pride, had put it simply in his famous address on "The New South" (1886): the New South had "fallen in love with work" (33, 38). This southern infatuation with work derived, according to Joel Williamson, from the lesson taught by the Civil War — that "industry and commerce were the keys to power, and power was what they wanted" (100). Atlanta played a major role in the southern march of progress, as a site of successful industrialization, as host city for two important cotton expositions (1881 and 1895), and as home of Grady, whose newspaper tirelessly advocated for southern growth and encouraged reunion with the capitalist North (Woodward, *Origins* 124; Frederickson 205; Berson 33; Doyle 158).

New South champions, as George Frederickson explains, tended to be at once antiaristocratic and deeply conservative, racially paternalistic and identified most of all with the emerging middle class (215). Although harboring few fantasies about the glory days of plantation life, leading proponents of the advancement of the New South envisioned a factory system that would incorporate Old South values. One major thread of this New South philosophy held that factories were for white people, while African Americans belonged on the land. Creating such a system, it was optimistically believed, would maintain plantation modes of control in the new context, and also keep poor whites and poor African Americans separate. The factory would be one kind of plantation, where the best whites could supervise the lower classes, while old forms of social control would continue to obtain in rural areas (Williamson 432). As Grady saw things, African Americans completely supported this aspect of the New South program: "No section shows a more prosperous laboring population than the negroes of the South, none in fuller sympathy with the employing and land-owning class" (34).

But the racial politics of the New South in general, and Atlanta most particularly, consistently gave the lie to Grady's hopeful vision. The Frank case came at the tail end of what Williamson has dubbed the radical era of southern politics, a defining feature of which was the intensification of racism in law and practice (181; see also Matthews 89; Dinnerstein 7–9). A major flashpoint for this deterioration in race relations was the construction of a nightmare vision of the "New Negro," an image rooted in the pseudoscientific belief that African Americans had, since Emancipation, been degenerating — reverting to type, as the lingo had it. This "New Negro" was fearsome, unruly, out for white women; in short he was wholly unlike the equally hypothetical "Old Negro" — the "Sambo" — of slavery days (Newby 125; Batteau 60, 94–95).

Atlanta was as much a trendsetter in race relations as it was in everything else in the postbellum South. If Booker T. Washington's famous "lay down your bucket" speech at the Atlanta Cotton States Exposition of 1895 marked his ascension to national leadership stature, then the Atlanta race riot of 1906, as Harlan notes, "showed that there was something systemically wrong with [his] formula for the assimilation of blacks into American society" (295). Major political battles had been fought over African Americans continually since the early years of the century; class arguments and rural/urban conflict were easily and effectively converted into a discussion about race (Lewis, *Du Bois* 334). A variety of reform movements coalesced in an effort to disfranchise African American voters, an achievement that was seen as a necessary pre-requisite for the adoption of prohibition in the city (Crowe, "Racial Violence" 237). Jews, who along with Greeks were highly visible as saloon owners, be-came conspicuous targets of prohibition efforts in the years after the riot. Calling African American customers "Mr." and "Mrs." might have seemed a harmless eccentricity in more peaceful times, but in the time of the riots this Jewish closeness to African Americans was transformed into a real threat (Hertzberg 161, 33).

The going proposition in Atlanta in these years was that all of the prob-lems of the city could be traced to the supposedly lazy and drunken African Americans hanging around Decatur Street bars; indeed, some accounts refer to Atlanta as the criminal capital of the United States during this era. But the coding of these African Americans as nonproductive could not hide the fact that white Atlantans were worried about the threatening labor reserve that African Americans represented. Nor could the emphasis on African Ameri-can vice conceal the integrated quality of the wickedness on Decatur Street (Lewis, *Du Bois* 334; see also Crowe, "Racial Violence" 248; Dittmer 124). Above all this rhetoric of African American criminality was linked to a repres-sive mode of labor supply, as Williamson demonstrates: "In 1905, out of about 80,000 whites and 50,000 blacks living in the city, Atlanta police made 17,000 arrests. Roughly 10,000 of those arrested were black men. Among those ar-rested, convictions ran high. Many of the convicts were leased out to the lum-ber companies, brickyards, and plantations around Atlanta, all of which were contributing to the city's prosperity. Attrition by death among the convicts was about 10 percent a year. Thus, in reality, black men were serving Atlanta very well indeed" (213). It is not hard to see, then, that the manipulation of racialized fear in Atlanta contributed to a variety of concrete New South objectives.

The most direct cause of the Atlanta Riot of 1906 was a hotly contested gubernatorial election in which race baiting became the central campaign modality. After the election the local newspapers kept up the attacks, paying special attention to a supposed increase of rapes committed by African American men. On September 22, the day of the riot, one paper printed five extras to announce the breaking news of additional rapes (Dittmer 124).[1] By about 9 o'clock that night the riot was in full effect. After a bloody Saturday night and quiet Sunday, the rioting spread to Brownsville, an African American suburb, on Monday. Although some attempt was made to pin blame for the riot on the lower classes, there is little doubt that the violence spread across all class lines (Williamson 222; Matthews 170). Fearing most of all for the credit rating of their city, Atlanta responded by organizing a Committee of Ten to address issues of racial concern in the city; one member was attorney Luther Z. Rosser who would go on to defend Leo Frank in 1913 (Baker 20). Responsible estimates put the total number of dead at around twenty-six: surely one of the strangest sights of the horrible strife came during the first flush of violence, when the dead bodies of three African Americans were carefully placed at the foot of a statue of Henry Grady, apostle of the New South (Dittmer 123–26; Crowe, "Racial Violence" and "Racial Massacre"; Lewis, *Du Bois* 334–37; Harlan 295–309; Williamson 209–23).

The riot was more or less a homegrown phenomenon. The murder of Mary Phagan, on the other hand, suggested that Atlanta had been opened up to malign foreign influences. Leo Frank was born in Texas but raised in Brooklyn and educated at Cornell University. Once arrested for the murder of Mary Phagan, Frank came to appear as a stereotypically exploitative Yankee/Jew. One detective who worked on the case argued that Frank's lynching "was a vicarious atonement for the rule of the carpetbagger in the South during the reconstruction period" and also claimed that Frank was easily recognizable to southerners as a "racial descendant of the carpetbaggers."[2] But Frank had surprisingly deep southern connections: his Uncle Moses, who recruited Leo to run the new pencil-making concern in Atlanta, was a Confederate veteran. After accepting Moses Frank's offer, Leo Frank went to Germany in 1907 to study pencil manufacturing, and then moved to Atlanta to take over the factory (Golden 6–8). Frank married Lucille Selig, the daughter of a prominent Atlanta family in 1911, and quickly became a leading member of Atlanta's Jewish community. As a successful and articulate German Jew, Frank certainly occupied a privileged place in Atlanta's Jewish community, which is not to say that he had much social currency among non-Jews. Luther Rosser, one of Frank's attorneys, overstated Frank's social marginalization but was close to the mark when he noted that the Jewish man had come "to Atlanta a stranger and engaged in a new enterprise. He knew hardly anybody who was not of his own religion, being clearly occupied with his business" (*New York Times,* 4 Mar. 1914: 2). Most descriptions of Frank from his own time to ours include references to his physical unattractiveness (with special mention for his bulging eyes, a common anti-Semitic caricature) and his nervous character. Taken together, these attributes are alleged to have kept Frank from becoming a successful salesman, not only in the strict business sense but also in a more diffuse way: Frank could not put himself over with the sort of grace that southerners reputedly held so dear (Golden 8; Dobkowski 48, 57).

It is worth stopping here to ask what sort of Jew Frank was, and what the implications of this status would be for southerners and other Americans who were observing his plight. To state the most obvious point, Frank was the kind of Jew who did not remember the Sabbath to keep it holy; he was working at the pencil factory on the Saturday when Mary Phagan was killed. Perhaps the most interesting evaluation of Frank's Jewishness is that found in the memoirs of Abraham Cahan, the great Jewish socialist, who visited Frank in prison in March 1914 and wrote a series of articles about the case for his Yiddish newspaper, the *Forward.* To introduce Frank to his readers Cahan called the jailed man an "authentic German Jew," using the word "yehudi" to describe him. In Hebrew "yehudi" simply means "Jew," but in Yiddish it means "Western Jew," and often carries a scornful tone. Addressing his heavily eastern European audience, Cahan noted that Frank's religious feeling apparently developed only in recent days, and in the manner of "Yehudim," not that "of our Jews" (Cahan 485). Frank's Jewishness was not only marked by its lack of religious ardor, he was also, as Cahan found him, uninterested in social questions. Unlike the imagined reader of the *Forward,* whose Jewish feeling encompassed religious and political commitment, Frank passively believed in the present social order simply because it existed (Cahan 485). (Cahan grew quite fond of Frank in his many visits to the jail; upon their parting, Cahan wished he could kiss the younger man in "our old-fashioned manner" but refrained because he knew that American men don't kiss like this [Cahan 537].)

The reform synagogue Frank belonged to also drew from a tradition in which good acts were supposed to accompany a belief in those aspects of Mosaic law that were in accord with the "views and habits of modern civilization." During Frank's years of membership the Hebrew Benevolent Congregation was led by Rabbi David Marx, a religious leader "committed to the survival of Judaism," but a Judaism "stripped of 'foreignism,' ritual, and formalism." Jews of this congregation generally eschewed wearing skullcaps and prayer shawls, eliminated the celebration of the bar mitzvah, referred to their place of worship as a "Jewish church," and reduced holiday observances to one day (Hertzberg 57, 69–71). In his novel about the Frank case, Richard Kluger parodies Rabbi Marx as Rabbi Weisz. (His last name itself a German joke about whiteness, Kluger's Rabbi embodies the old joke about the young boy who returns home from his first day at Trinity Day School and tells his father with great excitement what he learned at school: "God is in three parts," the little boy says, "the father, the son, and the holy ghost." The little boy's father grabs him sternly by the shoulders, looks him in the eye, and says, "Remember, son, there is only one God, and we don't believe in him.")

Atlanta had been a popular site for Jews to settle in the post-Reconstruction age: as an industrializing boom town it offered numerous opportunities for Jews with the right amount of capital or the right kind of goods. Although, as I have mentioned, Jews were implicated in the 1906 riot as purveyors of vice, in the years before the Frank case Atlanta appears to offer a prime demonstration of the "safe in America" thesis that has been put forth by Oscar Handlin and others to explain the level of comfort Jews have enjoyed here (Handlin; Moore, *At Home*).

The Frank case notwithstanding, southern Jews have experienced relatively little anti-Semitism. Here and there Jewish stores were attacked and verbal abuse was directed at Jews; the international power of Jewish finance was also an obsession for agrarian radicals. But the southern experience had been equally marked for Jews by philo-Semitism as it had been by sporadic examples of anti-Semitism; this fondness was at least partly due to comparisons between Jews and African Americans. Thomas Dixon, one of the more influential anti-Black racists of the Progressive Era, was enchanted by Jews, and noted that whenever anti-Semitism arose it was not because of the Jew's inferiority, "but because of his genius" (qtd. in Whitfield 87). Nathaniel Harris, who was governor of Georgia at the time of Frank's lynching, insisted that for "a man to be known as a Jew was actually an asset to him in a business way" (*New York Times*, 20 Aug. 1915: 4). Historical scholarship on American anti-Semitism is, as John Higham wrote some time ago, remarkably thin. What Higham does not mention is that all studies of American anti-Semitism are shadowed by questions of American exceptionalism: as with students of socialism in the United States, those interested in anti-Semitism in America must reckon with why there has been so little of it.[3]

Jews in southern cities were lodged in a social system intent on maintaining a strict Black/white division. As a result, Jews like Leo Frank were much more likely to take up whiteness as a self-concept and mode of behavior than their northern counterparts, for whom identification by intermediate racial categories was not only more available but also sometimes compulsory. The northern college quota crisis of the early 1920s, for instance, demonstrated in a fairly systemic way that Jews—in elite circles anyway—were considered to deviate from normative whiteness: after complaining about their exclusion from a junior prom at New York University, Jews were faced with a poster that read "Make New York University a White Man's College" (Dobkowski 167–68n67).

Leo Frank certainly felt "at home in America" and had no doubt that he was a white man who also happened to be Jewish. During his 1914 interviews with Cahan, Frank denied that his case bore any similarity to the contemporaneous ritual murder trial of Mendel Beilis in Russia, which was thick with anti-Semitic rhetoric: while Frank admitted that both cases were frame-ups, only Beilis's contained "authentic" anti-Semitism — the charge that Jews used the blood of Christian children to make their matzoh. His own case, Frank assured Cahan, was an example of random, improvisatory anti-Semitism (491).[4] Frank insisted that whatever anti-Semitism was directed at him only developed after the police, with no other handy suspects to harass, had built up a case against him. With an unintentionally revealing locution, Frank told Cahan that the police only began "to make capital" out of his origins once they had already turned the public tide of opinion against him as Mary Phagan's killer (488, 491). It is less interesting to note that Frank was wrong — of course the police had other potential villains to choose from — than to observe how much confidence Frank had that he possessed the social benefits of whiteness; in a letter written a bit over a month before his lynching, Frank wrote with much evident satisfaction that the "Warden [and] his staff have treated me white."[5] Frank explained to Cahan that the African American had no value in the South and was not to be believed against a white man. As a result, Frank thought his Jewishness had to be *added* to the public picture of him as a white man in order to make Conley's testimony more functional. A Jew, as Frank understood it, was not a southern Christian but still white (481). Cahan himself offered the opinion that once Conley's story had been established as the preferred version, southern whites had to rally against Frank because they could not let the rest of the world believe that an ignorant African American had misled them (508).

His wife, who also met with Cahan, seconded Frank's claims for his whiteness. Lucille Frank, speaking as a native southerner with inside information, reported to Cahan that southerners had always treated Jews as their "own kind" of people. Upon her husband's arrest the police were forced to circulate stories that highlight a type of perversion that might seem particularly Jewish; if they had not it might have become known that they were picking on an "innocent white man" as opposed to the available African American. With a stunning final flourish, Mrs. Frank declared to Cahan that if the situation had developed along these lines then the police themselves might have been in danger of being lynched (488)! Evoking the form of summary justice later applied to her husband, Lucille Frank reveals a tragically misguided pride of race.

If Frank *spoke* his whiteness unequivocally, he lived it in a more complicated fashion. Much about Frank's life signified his whiteness. The African
American servants who worked in the home he and his wife shared with her
parents, his control of poor African Americans and whites in the National
Pencil Company factory, and his conversion of an empty jail cell next to his
into a parlor to greet visitors, all indicated that Frank was a bourgeois white
man. In other ways Frank did not present a public image that matched pre-
vailing standards of white masculinity: one damaging failure came with Frank's
refusal of an offer made by Atlanta's chief of detectives to allow him to meet
with Jim Conley face to face during the initial investigation; the *Atlanta Constitution* wondered in a headline "Will Frank see the Negro?" (*Atlanta Constitution*, 30 May 1913: 2). Frank's unwillingness to meet with Conley was based
on a miscalculation of what a white man ought to do in this instance. While
Frank apparently thought it most prudent to draw attention to the social distance separating him from Conley, his decision instead conveyed the impression that Frank was a coward—that is, not much of a white man—and that
he did indeed have an intimate, if mysterious, relationship with Jim Conley.
Hugh Dorsey made much of this in his summation at the trial: "never in the
history of the Anglo-Saxon race," he argued, "never in the history of any other
race did an ignorant, filthy negro accuse a white man of a crime and that man
decline to face him" (Dorsey 99–100). Regardless of Frank's sense that "white"
was the primary category to explain his social position in southern life, his
public persona was shaped more by his departures from the ideals of whiteness. Such deviations were embodied especially in Frank's Jewishness, an identification woven out of both received images and newly minted concepts and
situated in a cultural field in which Jews were placed in a complex, defining
relationship with African Americans.

Even given the competition between African American and Jew in the
Frank case, it is still reasonable to ask why I focus my meditation on "Black-
Jewish relations" so morbidly, with one of the few lynchings of a Jew in United
States history? The most obvious reason is historiographical: the Frank case
has become a conventional starting point for studies of organized alliance building between African Americans and Jews. David Levering Lewis offers the
most influential claim for beginning inquiries into the subject with the Frank

case. In the Frank case Lewis discovers the moment when aloof and conservative Jewish leaders, shocked by the recognition that "an established Jewish merchant could be more vulnerable than a black janitor," belatedly threw in their lot with fellow-suffering African Americans ("Parallels" 547). Lewis makes a major contribution here to our understanding of how a very circumscribed enterprise (mostly the joint activity of advocacy groups) has come to stand for the entire shared landscape of African Americans and Jews; additionally, he reminds us that "Black-Jewish relations" should not be understood to refer to an equal partnership, or the natural result of historical parallels. The heart of liberal investment in the whole enterprise of Black-Jewish relations is the notion that because African Americans and Jews have been similarly oppressed throughout history, it was only a matter of time before each group, traveling along its discrete line, would look to the side, find a mirror image, and decide to make an alliance.[6] Of course this mixed metaphor underscores the problem with the model at its inception: parallel lines never meet. As Lewis so cogently argues on this point, the "predisposing factors of a vaguely kindred past and a similarly persecuted present lack the force of inevitability" ("Parallels" 547).

But if Lewis is correct to note that one *legacy* of the Frank case was to bring well-placed Jews and African Americans together, he ignores his own hint by leaving the case behind before coming to terms with what is to be found *within* it. In doing so, Lewis reproduces, albeit more critically than is usual, the dominant turn of surveys of Black-Jewish relations. This approach might best be described as a formalistic one, foregrounding organized, public moments of contact while erasing those broad and deep circumstantial contacts that have constituted the relationship.

In a pioneering essay published in *Phylon* in 1974, Eugene Levy offers an analysis of press reactions to the Frank case. Resisting the strong pressure toward Utopian revisionism that hampers most historians of Black-Jewish relations, Levy states outright that the complexities of reaction to Frank's tribulations derived from the fact that it was "the first well-focused incident of national interest in which the needs of blacks and of Jews seemed to have been in direct conflict." He demonstrates that African Americans, not without reason, "quickly came to feel that whites were again looking for a black scapegoat." Levy is admirably even-handed in his approach and recognizes that Jews were not alone in their less than noble response to the case: "Each group sensed its own weakness, and instinctively sought to offer up the other by emulating the prejudices of the majority" (212, 215, 222). Rather than simply marking a convenient point of origin for the onset of the construction of the grand alliance, then, 1915 will have to be replotted somewhere else on the graph (or else we will need to make a new graph).

Much of the energy of the Frank case was generated by the contest of African American and Jew *within* it; this compels us to reconsider whether any formal and universal condensation of the African American and Jewish relationship can maintain a meaningful relationship to the local expressions it purports to represent. This case provides a matchless example of how the veneer of similarity in the tribulations of Jews and African Americans often covers up exactly those differences that, after festering in a culture of avoidance, later proved fatal to the maintenance of untroubled notions of alliance. To say it another way, the Leo Frank case supplies an example of how African Americans and Jews have been *related*, but not simply as allies. In fact, the final part of this investigation of the Leo Frank affair argues that it was only after the lynching of Frank—and the attendant defusing and reconfiguration of Jewish concerns around the case—that scripts of Black-Jewish kinship came to prominence. Before this time the case was marked, as Levy demonstrates, by intense conflict between Jews and African Americans: not quite a zero-sum game of racial partisanship, but not so far off either.

The Frank case reveals that "Black-Jewish relations" retains its functional capacity only so long as we understand it as a container for an array of intersecting rhetorical economies, and not as a thing in itself. The most obvious way to demonstrate this is to examine the role played by southern whites in shaping the contest of African American versus Jew in and around the case. While Frank and Conley (and the African American and Jewish supporters of each) certainly played a large role in fashioning this public contest of Southern Others, the most influential interventions were made by Solicitor-General Hugh Dorsey and the former Populist leader Thomas Watson. This reveals to us that "Black-Jewish relations" is not executed in some sort of ethnic laboratory, free and clear of outside interference, but is staged in a public sphere in which the most powerful actors are often neither African American nor Jewish. The shaping role played by southern whites in the Frank case, *especially with reference to the relative positioning of Jews and African Americans*, also reminds us that "Black-white relations" predates "Black-Jewish relations" and that the latter must be appreciated as a relatively late addition to the history of the former. "Black-Jewish relations," in other words, is a language spoken by many who are not directly implicated by it.

For instance, the election of the southern Democrat Woodrow Wilson in 1912 has been posited by many historians as the climax of a decades-long process of reunion between northern and southern whites, a reunion that pointedly excluded African Americans. Disfranchisement, increased racial violence, a recrudescence of scientific racism, and Jim Crow laws and practices were all part of this social movement (Williamson 327–95). As early as 1888, former abolitionist Anna Dickinson complained that white northerners and southerners had been "grasping hands across the prostrate body of the negro" (Silber 157).

Frank's attorneys and his supporters all over the country confidently activated the rhetoric of national reunion in an attempt to clear their man; commentary on Black beast rapists, popular in this time when the "degeneration" of African Americans was widely agreed upon, became a familiar feature of pro-Frank discourse (Newby 48; Williamson 111). But the national trend toward reunion was overpowered in Atlanta by a more local form of consolidation, that between southern whites and African Americans. Playing out a plantation fantasy of powerful white masters and their loyal slaves, Atlantans generally resisted the movement toward national unity in the moment of the Frank case, opting instead for an older mode of social organization. Indeed, in Ward Greene's early fictionalization of the Frank case, the Jewishness of the villain — now a trade school teacher — is erased and his northern status is highlighted; in this way, the author Ward Greene quite appropriately underlines that sectional unification was, in fact, at issue in the Frank case. The opposition of national and regional in the Frank case should act as a reminder that while "Black-Jewish relations" has usually referred to a broad discourse of group relations, it has rarely been an effective predictor of local instances of intergroup activity. The Frank case calls into question how a partial narrative of alliance that was founded and mostly set in New York, has come to serve as the organizational idiom for every moment of African American-Jewish association.

There are other important ways in which the Frank case discloses the competing economies that structure "Black-Jewish relations." As we will see, one of the most striking aspects of the Frank case was how it challenged the seemingly predictable workings of power in southern society. As of April 25, 1913, Leo Frank was a fairly anonymous man, respected in his own small community but little-known outside of it. Jim Conley was similarly obscure, but already constituted as a particular type of "roustabout Negro" familiar (at least as fantasy figure) to white Atlantans. Beginning with Mary Phagan's murder on April 26, these two men would gradually be brought before the sight of the public, but not as might be expected. Before that date, Frank held enormous power over Conley and Mary Phagan, a power that would be demonstrated during and after the trial by Frank's enemies and by Frank himself: Frank considered himself to be white and enjoyed the privileges thereof, including African American domestic help and control over a large number of poor southerners—white and African American (Cahan 488). But Frank's power ultimately proved no match for the power accessed by Jim Conley. Jim Conley was described by one assistant to Hugh Dorsey as being as "sophisticated as Satan himself," and was able to translate the southern belief in the inferiority of the African American into a protective shield and an effective weapon; in short, for a brief time Conley was able to transform the usually oppressive racism of whites into a power greater than that of his boss at the factory (Golden 64). Here too the Frank case opens up a little-noted feature of "Black-Jewish relations": even as the success narrative of "Black-Jewish relations" has been rooted in the greater social and economic power of Jews, this does not cancel the enormous contribution made by the vast symbolic value of African Americans.

Finally, the Frank case uncovers in the most profound way imaginable that the canonization of "Black-Jewish relations" has depended on an elevation of a racial/historical likeness—at once gossamer-thin and definitive—that diverts attention from more divisive issues of class, gender, and sexuality. With Jim Conley and Leo Frank it proved impossible to promote the racial analogy with much force, because disparity in class status and affect offered up much more compelling grounds for comparison. Many people did see the persecution of Frank as proof of the similar social status of African Americans and Jews, but this formed a minority discourse of resemblance within a larger one of difference. In this respect the Frank case might tempt us to execute a simple reversal of the common moves that establish and maintain "Black-Jewish relations." Substituting class difference for racial similarity we might topple the rhetorical structure altogether.

The circumstances that pitted Leo Frank against Jim Conley extend the opportunity, however, for an even more satisfying inquiry, one that stitches race and class back together — along with sexuality and gender — in order to determine how each category of identity implicates and, in fact, helps create the others. In Leo Frank, we find a man whose public identity was overdetermined by the interplay of categories that too often are treated as autonomous social agents. The production of Frank's perversity in the case was dependent on related perceptions of his lack of manliness, his wealth/power, and his Jewishness, each of which came to appear as a natural cohort of the others, and all of which gained currency in their relation to Jim Conley's very different qualities. Abdul JanMohammed has recently argued that in studying historical issues surrounding sexuality, we must be sure to include what he calls "racialized sexuality": how racial Others get created through discussions of their sexuality. In the Frank case quite a lot of effort was made to define and indeed to "race" the sexualities of Leo Frank and Jim Conley: the coercive imputation of a sexuality to each man would have been impossible without drawing on available languages of class and race (JanMohammed 105). Frank's obvious class affect — unmistakably tied up with his Jewishness — made it difficult for participants in the trial to take part in the sort of rudimentary marginalizing rhetorics ("Black beast rapist," for instance) that likely would have become available if this had been a straightforward Black/white affair.

In short, the contest of sexual outsiders that distinguished the Frank case brings to light the impracticality of insisting that rigid boundaries divide the social workings of class, race, sexuality, and gender; social identities, we learn from the Frank case, must be appraised in all their complexity.[7] For Jim Conley, a precise sexual identity was more or less a ready-made, already available as the yield of centuries of white American erotic investment in the figure of the Black man. But the fairly straightforward models of white projection that have dominated study of the overlap of race and sex cannot explain why Conley's sexuality was enshrined as "natural" while Frank's was demonized as perverse. As the image of a Jewish capitalist came into focus over the course of the Frank trial, the sexuality of African Americans had to be revised in order to serve as the acceptable counterpoint to the forbidden behaviors ascribed to Frank. The introduction of Jews (and other white ethnics) as a major presence in the United States made it necessary to reconsider the simple binary opposition that pitted the sexual restraint thought to be central to white civilization against the alleged sexual licentiousness at the heart of African American savagery. Out of the Frank case a new math was devised—more of a continuum now than the unbridgeable Black/white chasm of earlier times— whereby sexuality ran from the unspoiled if oversexed African American, through the normative white American, and out the other side to the decadent, overcivilized Jew.

Whatever images of Jews had circulated in American society, few matched up in any deeply meaningful ways with the sexual violence done to Mary Phagan. As a number of Sander Gilman's books have made clear, Europeans have long indulged in a fascination with the Jew's sexuality. Although this practice became particularly intense in medical and literary discourses around the turn of the century, there is meager direct evidence that the public construction of Frank's perversion drew much from European models. A grab bag of racial and religious anti-Semitism formed the public view of Frank's sexuality, which was also created partly out of an inversion of convenient materials on Black sexuality, and out of more diffuse images of Jewish criminality and Jewish economic success in America. The Jew's body, to borrow a Gilman title, became in the Frank case a site for the working out of a variety of social questions, not the least important of which is what relation Jews and African Americans were to have with each other in America in general, and Atlanta more specifically. As such, what follows fastens on the perversion charge lodged against Frank in an attempt to understand how and why the enigmatic sexual violence done to a young southern white woman gave rise to such intense rituals of definition and ascription. To do so is to uncover valuable information about all manner of politics—from the sexual to the national—in the United States in the World War I era. It also quite consciously puts questions of sexuality back into Black-Jewish relations. In the Frank case the connections between sexuality and violence were plain, and inspired a variety of discourses concerned with the relative power of Jews, African Americans, and southern whites.

The seemingly irrational response of certain powerful white southerners to the murder of Mary Phagan should be understood as a strategy meant to correct an imbalance in social relations caused by decades of rampant industrialization and urbanization in the New South; the Frank case helps us see how truly frightening these twin processes were. The discovery of the dead body of a young white woman in a factory owned by Jews offered up a significant opportunity to address some big problems in Atlanta—perhaps most notably that when New South leaders invited northern capital into the post-Reconstruction South they did not reckon fully with the reality that along with northern capital comes northern capitalists. The presence of Jewish capitalists (and even small-scale merchants) in Atlanta and other New South cities upset the racial applecart that Jim Crow laws had helped to set in place in the 1890s and after. The Frank case—along with the riot of 1906—represented an impromptu and hysterical effort on the part of influential Atlantans to redraw the racial landscape of their city. Calling Leo Frank a pervert was remarkably apt shorthand for describing all of Atlanta's problems in these years.

"FRANK ON
HIS KNEES"

Capitalism and Perversion in the New South

The perversion charge merits special attention because it formed the emotional core of the prosecution's case against Frank, and also became the most important constituent in public feeling against him. The issue of Frank's "perversion" also extends an opportunity to explore the often uncomfortable and certainly unacknowledged differences in the ways Jews and African Americans have been objectified. Similarly, it will suggest one approach for understanding the complicated nature of Jewish/African American relatedness at this eminently plausible point of origin. It is with the perversion charges made against Frank that we can see most clearly how an insistence upon a relationship between an African American and a Jew — perhaps one that itself was partly imaginary — could be used to marginalize both groups, even as its most direct effect was to criminalize the Jewish capitalist.

Leo Frank was hardly the alien Jew who dominates most historical scholarship on the case; rather, even while his precise social role was obscure and his demeanor inscrutable, Frank was all too recognizable in his role as factory boss. What needs to be examined critically is how Frank's familiar enough class position became intertwined with his Jewishness and was channeled through an accusation that he was a pervert. It is within this very process of naming that the central drama of the Frank case — the encounter of Jew and African American over the body of a dead white woman — was played out.

Some accounts of the Frank case have made distinctions between Frank's Jewishness on the one hand and the charges of perversion on the other (Freshman 52; Lindemann 237–40). My claim here will be that the two, along with his status as a "damnyankee" capitalist from New York are of a piece (White, *Man* 25). The specific form that the perversion charges took, I will assert, were dependent on Frank's image as a Jewish capitalist. Frank's position in the economic and moral body of the South was almost completely coded through the attribution of a complicated sexual persona to him that repelled observers even as it inspired in them an obsessive interest in the particularities of his deviance. Above all, the allegations of perversion made against Frank suggested a determining contrast between this Jewish manager and the African American janitor who provided the charges against him. While the comparison profited the latter in the short run — and perhaps saved his life — the broader point to make is that it also posited the public identities of African American and Jew as equally divergent from normative whiteness. The ultimate effect of the perversion charges was to position African Americans and Jews as distorted reflections of each other: the supposedly "instinctual" behaviors of Conley, that is, came to be seen as the relatively healthy opposite of the image of Frank as cultured to the point of decay.

The centerpiece of the perversion charge, that Frank coerced southern white women to have oral sex performed on them because he was not "built like other men," compels a reconsideration of sociological theories of labeling and scapegoating, particularly those that address racism and anti-Semitism. American sociology had a sort of golden age of deviancy studies in the 1950s and 1960s with influential works by Howard Becker and Kai Erikson, among others, establishing an explanatory model that insisted that the construction of deviancy played a major role in society building. Arguing against the long-held idea that deviance is an inherent quality, Becker noted that social groups *make* deviance and proposed the now-familiar axiom that "deviant behavior is behavior that people so label" (9). Erikson pushed this insight further, arguing that it is "deviancy" that makes group life possible: to Erikson the deviant is "a relevant figure in the community's overall division of labor" whose punishment gives the rest of society an "orderly sense of their own cultural identity" (4, 9, 13; see also Cohen 193).

But how are particular scapegoats chosen? Rene Girard proposes that a fairly free hand can be used in choosing a scapegoat, but that real care must be taken to "cultivate the future victim's supposed potential for evil, to transform him into a monster." If this is successfully done the scapegoat can hold "all the infectious strains in the community": killing the scapegoat means curing the social body at large (Girard, *Violence* 107). Girard has more recently called attention to how a potential victim becomes suspect by appearing to be ready-made, attracting catastrophe, that is, simply by bearing the marks of victimhood (*Scapegoat* 72).

But of course "looking like" a scapegoat implies a process by which an available subject is interpreted to be an appropriate match — the right villain — for the crime committed. Here the judging society tends to examine the potential sacrifice for "a single cue or a small number of cues in actual, suspected, or alleged behavior" that distinguish him or her as "the kind of person" who could have been responsible for the original transgression (Schur 52; Erikson 7). Since, as Erikson has written, deviancy appears exactly where it is has been feared the most, it is not difficult to understand how, in the Frank affair, the man controlling the bodies of young southern women (as well as those of African Americans) would come to light as a perfect scapegoat for the murder of Mary Phagan (22).

In fact, just such an interpretation has dominated analysis of the Frank case. The dominant explanation goes something like this: Atlantans saw in the murder of Mary Phagan the embodiment of everything that was wrong about New South industrialism; not only had African Americans become idle and unmanageable, but foreigners, mostly Jews, were taking control over local commerce — just as they had already come to dominate international finance. Faced with the appalling crime and its strange details, southerners scapegoated Leo Frank, holding him responsible for the entire burden of post-Civil War southern history.[1]

The seductive logic of all this should not obscure its shortcomings. Even if deviancy theory can help us to explain why Leo Frank was chosen over Jim Conley to be punished for Mary Phagan's murder, it offers little help in describing how the rhetorical attack on Frank came to have its effectiveness. Charles Herbert Stember has wisely criticized one branch of scapegoat theory that holds that stigmatizing of outgroups generally follows either an "id" ascriptive pattern (lazy, oversexed, ignorant, dirty) or a "superego" pattern (acquisitive, pushy, shrewd). Imagining projection as a hydraulic system, this model does not advance our understanding of how more complicated labels are created and applied (Stember 49–50). In short, simply classifying Leo Frank as a scapegoat cannot account for the specific form of the perversion charges made against him, nor can it explain the concomitant designation of Jim Conley's sexuality as relatively benign.

Melvin Tumin suggests that stereotypes, though largely false, "have the advantage of simplicity" (14). But the construction of the perversions assigned to Frank can hardly be said to be simple. Nor can it easily be argued that the "deviant" acts imputed to Frank represented behavior that was craved by those making the charges, as some scapegoat theorists would put it (Cohen 190); for one thing, cunnilingus simply was not on the map in a clear enough form for it to signify in a direct way for observers at the time of Frank's trial. Nevertheless, if the accusation that Frank performed cunnilingus in the factory has confusing local meanings, its general relevance, as Nancy MacLean has made clear, cannot be overlooked: Frank was being accused of taking control over southern women. With this it might do to consider the contribution made by H. Dieter Seibel to deviance theory. According to Seibel, no deviant acts "can be committed between units that do not stand in a social relationship to each other. Without a social relationship, there is no need for social integration; without a need for social integration, there is no need for deviance" (277–78).

There is little doubt that Frank's status as a capitalist roused great enmity during the trial and after, and that the specific conceptions that circulated were inseparable from the negative connotations surrounding his Jewishness.[2] The Atlanta *Journal of Labor* put it most directly at the time, writing that "Mary Phagan [was] a martyr to the greed for gain which has grown up in our complex civilization, and which sees in the girls and children merely a source of exploitation" (qtd. in Dinnerstein 10; see also Connolly 27). An African American newspaper commented that "through the relationship" of employer and employee, Mary Phagan "could easily have been at [Frank's] mercy" (*Indianapolis Freeman*, 21 Aug. 1915: 4). The historian Nancy MacLean has perceptively read one meaning of the anti-Semitism in this case as a simple answer "for the complicated questions of changing patterns of class, power and female sexuality" that accompanied industrialization. I think, however, that she might oversimplify when she goes on to argue that to observers of the case "capitalism was a good social system, unless manipulated and deformed by Jews," because in the atmosphere surrounding the Frank case, to speak of capitalists was, ipso facto, to speak of Jews (MacLean 942).

Most students of this case have assiduously drawn the connections between Frank's appeal as a villain and his position in the employing class, so I will rehearse the outlines of this argument only briefly. The first scholarly account of the case, by Leonard Dinnerstein (1968), held that "Leo Frank was chosen to stand trial for the tribulations of a changing society." Dinnerstein admits the sexual dimension of the disruption by quoting a mill owner who reported that "to let a girl go into a cotton factory was to make a prostitute of her," but never follows up on this point (ix, 10). In his groundbreaking book *Strangers in the Land* (1963), John Higham makes the connection more explicit with a brief summary of the case. He writes that "unsubstantiated rumors of sexual perversion helped to fix suspicion on Frank. Most aroused were the working classes, who saw in Frank a symbol of the northern capitalist exploiting Southern womanhood" (185). In a popular account of the case, Harry Golden comes to the same conclusion. Golden even quotes a flyer distributed at the time that read "Buy your clothing from Americans. Don't give your money to save a Jew Sodomite"; still he refuses to draw precise connections between the anti-Semitic and anti-capitalist sentiments and the fear of sexual corruption (209, 223). And Nancy MacLean, who finally gives the gender power relations that reside in this case their due, downplays the Jewish question in order to do so.[3]

Anti-capitalist and anti-Jewish sentiments became most shrill around the issue of Governor John Slaton's commutation of Frank's death sentence. In the two years between Frank's trial and his lynching, concerns were raised, not surprisingly (and not without some basis), about the huge amount of money and effort expended on his behalf. Many observers, in fact, attributed whatever anti-Semitism surrounded the Frank case to the manipulative actions of a "Hebrew cabal" that was funding Frank's defense. According to a history of Georgia published in 1917, it was Jews "binding themselves together to accomplish Frank's rescue" who were responsible for supplying "fuel to an anti-Semitic feeling, causing it to spring eventually into an open flame of race hatred" (Knight 1165–66; Busch 15).[4] Outside of Georgia most major newspapers supported the drive for a new trial for Frank, and many wealthy and powerful Americans lined up in support of Frank.[5] One old friend of Frank suggested to the condemned man that it might be time to drive northern capital out of Georgia and "depreciate their bonds" if they remained recalcitrant.[6]

When Slaton finally did commute the sentence, a hue and cry about Jewish bribe money and Jewish conspiracies was raised. Many incensed letter writers accused Slaton of selling out, as this Georgian did: "You have saved your lodge brother rapist and murderer of little girls.... Oh you rat souled spawn of a filthy degenerate breed, if you have daughters of your own, may you feel what the parents of poor little Mary Phagan have felt.... [T]he good people of the Soverign [sic] State of Georgia, should crucify you along with that low skunk white livered hell hound defiler and murderer of infants Frank, upon a gibbett [sic] of Oak.... Go with your filthy Jew bribe money and may you be a branded wanderer upon the face of the earth."[7]

This confusion of explicitly classical anti-Semitism ("murderer of infants" being an obvious blood libel reference), with economic and racial anti-Semitism (captured in the one phrase "lodge brother rapist") was uncommon in the case, but the notion that Frank was now symbolically corrupting the entire body politic of the South after having already defiled one of its female members was an oft-repeated claim. In the contested moral universe created by the fallout of the case, one well-off southern woman could write to Slaton with great anger and no discernible irony that it "was *money* against honor and 'money' weighed heavier. During your last campaign I had our tenants with my husband stop their farm work to go vote for you."[8] As with most lynchings of "white" people in the South, a loss of faith in the orderly workings of the legal system preceded the appeal to summary justice (Brundage 87): in Frank's case it seemed obvious to many that the immense power of international Jewry would see clear to freeing the murderer of Mary Phagan. The earliest reports of Frank's abduction from prison in August 1917, in fact, repeated a rumor that he had been seized by friends who had attacked the prison in order to liberate the Jewish prisoner; even after the news of Frank's lynching spread throughout the nation, one Georgia newspaper reported that there were local people who still held to the belief that the "lynching of Leo Frank...was a faked affair, and that he was spirited away to freedom by his friends" (*New York Times*, 17 Aug. 1915: 1).

It might be worth posing a general question, asked recently by Albert Lindemann: How was Frank "transformed in the public eye from respected businessman and community leader to loathsome murderer and sexual pervert"? (238). One obvious answer is that Frank never existed in the public eye as a "respected businessman and community leader." As superintendent of the pencil factory, Frank was mostly concerned with behind the scenes work — accounting, purchasing, and the like — and not with sales or public relations. Similarly, as president of Atlanta's B'nai B'rith (which is, I assume, what Lindemann is referring to here in calling Frank a community leader), Frank would have been relatively invisible to the general population of the city. Kai Erikson argues that to sanction a deviant the surrounding society must undertake "an intricate rite of transition" that moves "the individual out of his ordinary place in society" and places him in the deviant category (15). Since Frank had no individual public image before the murder of Mary Phagan — and given my contention that the categories of Jew, capitalist, and pervert were complexly entwined in this case — I think it might be more helpful to reformulate Lindemann's question to ask more simply: How was Frank's Jewishness brought to light? And to what effect?

Before turning to the public consciousness of Frank's race, we must first attend to the features of his face. Late in 1914 or early in 1915 an Atlanta newspaperman sent his impressions of Leo Frank's case to a concerned northern Jew, perhaps the philanthropist Julius Rosenwald. He wrote: "If you have seen any good pictures of him [Frank], you will understand what I mean when I say that he looks like a pervert. It is a slightly significant fact, I think, that I sized him up as one the first time I saw him, before a whisper of the perversion testimony came out" (qtd. in Dinnerstein 172–77). This correspondent would also claim that there was little anti-Semitism manifested in the case, if any. But an acknowledgment that Frank was different, and not in any good way, became a central constituent in the case built against him. In Albert Lindemann's recent history of the case, he has this to say about the handicaps Frank faced at the trial: "Frank had another problem . . . difficult to evaluate but impossible to ignore: He was physically unattractive or at least unimpressive and odd looking in terms of southern models of manhood. It may simply have been that Frank was unphotogenic . . . but his odd physical qualities would be the source of much comment, even among those who watched him daily during the trial. . . . Frank's physical appearance unquestionably helped many to view him as alien and capable of heinous acts." What was so odd about Frank's looks? Lindemann describes him as having been "five feet six inches tall, thin, with thick lips, thick glasses, and bulging eyes" (243–44). This last detail, as I have mentioned, is a stock anti-Semitic image: Sander Gilman has located references to the "goggle" eyes of the Jew in many European sources (*Jew's Body* 68–72). While the thick lips might suggest a confusion of Jew and African American, this description of Frank more directly taps into available popular imagery surrounding the Jewish satyr. More important yet, the attention drawn to Frank's lips by Tom Watson among other observers of the trial was intended, no doubt, to feminize the Jewish man as well. If Frank's mouth was, on the one hand, his tool for violating the virginal Mary Phagan, the lips also came to stand for Frank's likeness to a woman: since the perversion case depended on the charge that Frank was not "built like other men," the central site of his sexuality was moved from his genitals toward his mouth, which then came to be pictured as an analogue of female genitalia.[9]

For his part, Albert Lindemann, in his attempt to downplay the influence of anti-Semitism in the Frank affair, goes on to offer this clincher: "Whether or not his physical and mental traits meant that he 'looked Jewish' or 'acted like a Jew' may certainly be questioned, for other prominent Jews in town did not look or act that way. . . . If Frank had seemed less a distant and superior outsider, if he had been a more familiar type . . . then matters might have developed differently." "In short," Lindemann concludes, "if a different Jew had been in . . . Frank's . . . position, a different course of events might have occurred" (243–44). Much of this reasoning belongs to the "if my grandmother had wheels she would be a trolley" school. Frank did seem like an outsider and he was not a familiar "type." One likely explanation for this is that Jews in Atlanta, primarily of German heritage, and Reform religious practices, had assimilated in an enormously successful fashion. If other "prominent Jews in town did not look or act that way" it was because they had either passively lost or consciously and voluntarily surrendered their ethnic/religious particularity for the perceived comfort that invisibility would afford.[10]

In Lindemann's description it is plain that Frank had physical traits that matched exaggerated components of racial (as opposed to religious) anti-Semitism.[11] Testimony during the trial mentioned such marked characteristics as Frank's "shifty" nature, his tendency to rub his hands together nervously, and his "large" and "funny" eyes. In Frank's time these traits circulated most especially in popular culture — on the vaudeville stage, in the presentation of the "Jew Comic," and in movies. In a 1922 film version of *Oliver Twist*, for instance, Lon Chaney, playing Fagin, rubs his hands together every time money is mentioned (Golden 228; Dinnerstein 41; Friedman 18).[12] Nancy MacLean has recently repeated Harry Golden's fascinating suggestion that *Watson's Magazine* retouched a photo of Frank to accent just those features that made him seem most foreign. Racial and religious anti-Semitism were always in competition with what has been called southern "philosemitism," so it was still possible to think of "good" Jews and "bad" Jews, of which Frank was certainly the latter.[13] Lurking beneath my discussion here (and embedded in the discourse surrounding the trial) is one essential question, posed first by Robert Abbott of the *Chicago Defender,* and used later by Eugene Levy for the title of his article on this case: Is the Jew a white man?[14]

Once Frank was arrested there must have been available images that the public accessed in forming opinions about him. What experience did Atlantans have that would allow them to imagine Frank as a capitalist/Jew/pervert? Interestingly, one of the primary negative images of Jews in Atlanta derived from their willingness to interact with African Americans. According to a *New York Times* article of the time, Atlantans hated all foreigners, because they refused to make a distinction between Black and white (qtd. in Levy 215). Steven Hertzberg, a historian of Jewish life in Atlanta, explains that of necessity the city's Russian Jews "were compelled to court the patronage of those whose business was scorned by more established merchants." Although Hertzberg describes such business as being at the most "stigmatized" level, he also notes that the recently arrived immigrants "had few if any temperamental objections to dealing with blacks, and, unlike their white gentile counterparts, had no deep-seated compulsion to manifest anti-Negro prejudice." Quite to the contrary, Russian Jews, particularly those running pawnshops and saloons, actively sought the custom of African Americans (184–85; see also Lindemann 232). Jews were also implicated in the operation of brothels, gambling dens, and "dope dives." The operation of saloons created special problems. Leonard Dinnerstein reports that "sensual pictures of nude white women allegedly decorated the walls of many of these establishments, and rumors circulated that even the labels on the liquor bottles were designed to incite Negro passions" (71). Abraham Cahan, for one, believed that the root of all the perversion imagery surrounding Frank was the actual fact that a portrait of a beautiful woman hung on a door of the factory (383).

The attachment of these negative images is surprising because these biases usually attached to Russian Jews, and not well-established German Jews like Frank; in his novel *Members of the Tribe*, Richard Kluger responds to this social confusion logically by transforming Leo Frank into a Polish Jew named Noah Berg (formerly Berkowitz). Additionally, for all the hysterical distancing strategies employed by the African Americans and Jews involved in this case, they could not escape the established connection that had Jews serving, more or less, as purveyors of vice for African American men. It is likely that particular impressions of Leo Frank imperceptibly meshed with these existing prejudices.

The historian Nancy MacLean has written recently that while Frank "stood trial on the charge of murder alone, the allegation that he had raped Mary Phagan became the centerpiece of the case against him," even though medical examiners "never found clear evidence of rape" (918, 936). MacLean is certainly correct to emphasize the sexual component of the case against Frank, but I think she stops short of a completely satisfying understanding of just what was being charged against Frank. In fact, the absence of medical evidence (trauma to the genitalia, for instance) is what made it possible for so many to project fantasies of evil onto Frank.

Frank himself was aware of the central role the perversion charges played in his conviction. In a public statement published in the *Atlanta Journal* after his trial, Frank addressed the issue with a rhetorical question: "Is there a man in Atlanta...who would deny that the charge of perversion was the chief cause of my conviction, or deny that the case, without that charge, would be an entirely different question" (qtd. in Dinnerstein 102). Twenty factory workers testified during the trial to Frank's generally lascivious behavior, which included peeping into the women's changing room and touching them in a sexual way. Frank himself explicitly denied "making improper gaze" during the statement he delivered at his trial but admitted having to look into the changing room occasionally to spy on workers (Kean 140; *Brief of Evidence* at 219).[15] As the Frank affair wore on, the spying charges might have come to be particularly irksome to working-class Atlantans, some of whom had been under surveillance — by William J. Burns, whom Frank also hired as his own private detective — during the Fulton mill strike that began in 1914 (Hall, "Private Eyes").

Kathy Peiss has recently noted that many factories of this era "lacked privacy in dressing facilities and workers tolerated a degree of familiarity and roughhousing between men and women" (61). But whether common or not, Leo Frank's admission of what Ishmael Reed calls "reckless eyeballing" could not have helped his case; if anything, it served to remind all observers just how great his power was in the factory. Leslie Fiedler nicely captures the emotional urgency of the snooping charge. As Fiedler puts it, Leo Frank

> was clearly identified as a "capitalist," doubly a capitalist, since to the *lumpen* Socialist mind of the American Populist capitalist equals Jew, and the two together add up to demidevil. And in certain regards, the record seems to bear them out; for Frank did hire child labor, did work it disgracefully long hours at pitifully low wages; and if he did not (as popular fancy imagined) exploit his girls sexually, he walked in on their privacy with utter contempt for their dignity. Like most factory managers of the time, he was — metaphorically at least — screwing little girls like Mary Phagan. (Fiedler 135)

Other innuendoes, some introduced by Hugh Dorsey, some by witnesses, suggested that Frank had "clandestine trysts with prostitutes" and "homosexual liaisons," and that he "engaged in sexual acts with his nose" (MacLean 932; Dinnerstein 17–19, 51). Where did these claims of perversion come from? Many were productions of what Jacquelyn Dowd Hall has termed "folk pornography": such productions of public fantasies surrounding sex crimes have the obvious aim of defusing anxiety by describing a relatively coherent version of events that offer up a recognizably monstrous villain — the "ravenous brute" — attacking a "frail young virgin." Usually, the verbal reenactments of such scenes offer pleasures to already powerful people — in this case, white men (Hall, *Revolt* 150). Atlanta newspapers, involved in a major circulation war at the time of the Frank case, were the source for some of the most pernicious rumors; the papers reproduced uncritically all the information that was strategically being leaked by the Atlanta police who were thus building up a case against Frank in the public imagination. One key piece of information that helped criminalize Frank was provided by brothel madam Nina Formby, who told the police not only that Frank was a frequent visitor to her establishment but also that his tastes were perverse (Cahan 380). The specific Jewish angle of the charges made against Frank was noted by C. P. Connolly, who covered the trial for *Collier's*. According to Connolly, "one of the stories most religiously circulated by well-meaning and highly respected citizens of Atlanta...was that the tenets of the Jewish faith forbade the violation of a Jewess but condoned that of a Christian woman" (14). The credibility of this last assertion had been established by the influential sociologist Edward A. Ross, who included it in his 1914 book *The Old World in the New* as part of a general attack on the malfeasance of Jews: "The fact that pleasure-loving Jewish business men spare Jewesses but pursue Gentile girls excites bitter comment" (150; see also Samuels and Samuels 21). As early as 1888 one anti-Semite had complained that in "many of the factories operated by the Jews throughout the country, the life of an honest girl therein employed is made simply a hell, by reason of the Jew's predominant lechery" (qtd. in Selzer 53). Nancy MacLean has argued that within the Frank case such general claims about Jews "aggravated the popular outrage the testimony itself elicited" and spoke to concerns about "loss of control and impending chaos" in the industrializing South (932). During the trial the defense allowed these claims to go unchallenged, which led many to assume their veracity; as a last-ditch effort, which reflected badly on their client, Frank's lawyers attempted to have all testimony on his perversion struck from the record as immaterial (Dinnerstein 46).

Contending with the negative images of Frank, I should note, were various positive ones, many of which were similarly overstated. As Clark Freshman has written in his fine study of the case, "like any martyr, Leo Frank had to be pure for his supporters"—as pure as his opponents needed him to be evil (57). Many of Frank's champions steeped their arguments in comparisons to Jim Conley. One man, a self-proclaimed phrenologist (phrenology was a racist vogue during the nineteenth century whose practitioners claimed they could "read" the bumps on human heads to learn about individual tempera-ment *and* the character of races), took up Frank's case in a letter to the Jewish man: "I have carefully studied your picture from a purely scientific standpoint and I fail to note any thing about your head [or] face that would justify the be-lief that you would, or could be guilty of the heinous crime. . . . I believe that the real murderer was a nig."[16]

Another concerned citizen wrote to President Woodrow Wilson that Frank, a "clean looking man" was not "likely to see much in a bit of a factory girl . . . more especially when he had a young attractive wife who could give him all the female attention and pleasure that he could possibly want." This letter goes on to suggest that the "black fellow" should be "put through what they call the third degree" in order to exonerate Frank.[17] Antagonistic attempts to vindicate Frank by implicating Conley led from one trap to another. To do so ultimately validated the process of racial scapegoating itself.

Although the sexual aspect of the crime against Mary Phagan was never an official constituent of the state of Georgia's case, it did receive intense scrutiny from all manner of observers. There were two general ways of thinking about the sexual violence that few doubted was the root cause of this murder. First, predictably and almost reflexively, came the claim that such an attack on an innocent white girl could only have been perpetrated by an African Ameri-can, as opposed to a white man; in these arguments, Frank's particular iden-tity as a Jew was generally ignored.[18] Second, and more interesting, were those who protested that the particulars of this "perverse" attack could not have been dreamed up by an instinctual African American and must have been the work of a decadent Jew.

The first structure, a revival of the myth of the Black rapist, was simple in its contours and implications. Perhaps the only very interesting thing about this line of thinking is the shocking absence of self-consciousness on the part of its propagators: numerous and varied supporters of Frank proved willing to employ racist thinking to condemn Jim Conley while often simultaneously decrying the similar sentiments that contributed to Frank's conviction. Isaac Gibson wrote to Governor Slaton to remind him that "the crime is one almost wholly confined in the South to the negro race against white girls"; like most observers this writer purposefully ignored the fact that the main story in the history of rape in the South had to do with the rape of African American women by white men.[19] New Hampshire's *Manchester Union* reminded its readers that not only was Jim Conley "known to be highly lecherous and morally depraved" but that the crime itself "was one peculiarly characteristic of the low-grade negroes of his kind."[20]

The years from 1913 to 1915 were ripe ones for reactivating fears about Black rapists. The year of Frank's lynching also saw the release of D. W. Griffith's *Birth of a Nation*, an epic whose emotional effect relied in large part on the audience's understanding of the danger posed by the uncontrolled lust of Black men, and a movie which found official sanction from the highest authority in the land: Woodrow Wilson is reputed to have exclaimed that Griffith's enormous achievement was "like writing history with lightning!" (qtd. in Bogle 10).[21] One of the key scenes of the movie depicted in its basic outlines the story of Mary Phagan as imagined by many: in *Birth of a Nation*, a young woman leaps to her death rather than submit to the desires of a threatening African American man. *Birth of a Nation* envisioned a time when social order had dissolved in the mixed blessing of emancipation, and, as Woodrow Wilson put it in his history of America, the "country was filled with vagrants looking for pleasure and gratuitous fortune" (qtd. in Rogin 348). The remedy for this anarchy, according to Griffith, came with the control imposed by the Ku Klux Klan.

Those who defended Leo Frank on racial grounds partook, then, in the same project as Griffith by equating evil with Black lust. A very few African American newspapers found connections between this movie (and the furor surrounding it) and the Leo Frank case — observations I will return to later. But there is a breathtaking irony embedded in the juxtaposition of these two events: in defending their man by appealing to fears of the Black rapist, Frank's reactionary supporters tapped into the same racist vein as Griffith's movie, but it was the success of this movie along with the excitement generated by the lynching of Frank that materially led to the formation of a new Ku Klux Klan (Dinnerstein 149–50).[22] Even more pointedly, the impulse behind reconstructions of the Black rapist in the person of Jim Conley proved unreliable when put into practice. At this time and in this place the mechanism for projecting a dangerous Otherness could be pointed toward a Jewish "pervert" with as much, if not more, effectiveness as if an African American "rapist" were the object.

What is most disturbing about the projections of Black rapists as the only possible villains in the Mary Phagan murder case is that many of them were explicitly authored by Frank's attorneys. While the fiction of the Black rapist existed well before the public ever heard of Leo Frank or Jim Conley, and probably would have attached to the case no matter what, it remains surprising to find this language in attorney Reuben Arnold's summation at Frank's original trial: "After Mary got her pay there was a black spider waiting for her down there near the elevator shaft, a great, passionate, lustful animal. . . . He was as full of vile lust as he was of the passion for more whiskey." Arnold went on to generalize about African Americans, raising a fear that "there are a thousand of them in Atlanta who would assault a white woman if they had a chance and knew they wouldn't get caught" (qtd. in Samuels and Samuels 157–58). Another of Frank's lawyers referred to Conley as a "dirty, filthy, black, drunken, lying nigger" and Frank himself damned Conley's testimony as the "perjured vaporizings of a black brute" (qtd. in Levy 214).

Frank's representative at his commutation hearing before Governor Slaton was somewhat subtler, and considerably more astute than Reuben Arnold had been in his understanding of the actual, if hidden, terms of contention at Frank's original trial. This attorney explained to Governor Slaton that the perversion charge was crafted specifically to debase Frank in "the public estimation, and [place] him on a level below that of the negro himself, and therefore make plausible" all the claims made by Conley about Frank.[23] Attorney Howard was savvy enough to explain first why the insinuations were made against Frank; he then went on to shift the blame to Conley. He did this by pointing back to the physical evidence of Mary Phagan's body, which in Howard's interpretation, showed the signs of intercourse "naturally done." He went on to suggest that "if Conley had been going to take advantage of a female forcibly and against her will, he would have done it in a normal and natural way," without explaining why this was necessarily so.[24] Howard here cleverly attempted to hang Solicitor-General Dorsey with his own rope by uttering the simple fact that Mary Phagan's body showed evidence of a rape done in a "normal and natural way." The conclusion he left Governor Slaton to make is that if this was a recognizable rape, than there was a more conventional suspect to be found than Leo Frank.[25]

Before moving on to the more complex effort made by opponents of Frank to produce a competing image of the sexual dimension of this crime so as to implicate Frank (or at least to clear Conley), it is worth asking why so many dwelt on the indecorous and anxiety-producing vision of a helpless factory girl being preyed on by a lustful man. After all, there was little positive evidence offered at the trial to suggest Phagan had been raped: one doctor "discovered no violence to the parts" and another saw no spermatozoa near or injury to her genitalia (*Brief of Evidence* at 46). The question of why so many insisted on the sexual constituent of the violence done to Mary Phagan is suggested in the ambiguity of this expert testimony, and is summarized persuasively by Nancy MacLean: "The belief that Mary Phagan was raped by Leo Frank rather than robbed by Jim Conley can be read in part as a massive exercise in denial on the part of people unwilling to acknowledge youthful female sexual agency. For although there was no compelling evidence of recent or forcible intercourse, there were physical signs that Phagan may not have been a virgin. Once her body had been found and examined, there were two choices: to believe that she had been murdered to cover up a perverse sexual assault that failed to leave the normal evidence or to admit that perhaps she had been sexually active before the day she was murdered and come to terms with the new social reality this scenario represented" (347). MacLean's careful summary of the sexual threats embodied by the factory murder of Mary Phagan were expressed years earlier by Richard Kluger, who imagines in his novel *Members of the Tribe* that Phagan, by age fourteen, had already been sexually assaulted by a variety of men — including her stepfather and an older man at the factory. But MacLean's point gives the lie to Kluger's suspect version: for powerful southerners like Hugh Dorsey and Tom Watson, the worst-case scenario of factory life is that it would grant young southern women a large degree of power to choose how to express their own sexuality.

Those who asserted that it was necessary to find a criminal "larger" than the average friendless African American rapist were somewhat off the mark; what was really needed was a crime larger than the average. The spectacle of Frank's malfeasance offered a panorama of horror that addressed in a more complete way the multiple hurts inflicted on Mary Phagan (and by extension all southern whites) than the vision of an African American rapist could (Girard, *Violence* 18).

The crime that usually haunted white southerners, the rape of white women by African American men, spoke to relatively straightforward anxieties about the power of unbridled lust — usually and mostly that of the white men who were doing the projecting of it (Williamson 306–10). Joel Williamson argues that in the years leading up to Mary Phagan's murder the image of the Black beast rapist had begun to give way to a "neo-Sambo" construction that described African Americans as docile and in need of the careful guidance of southern whites; furthermore, Williamson writes, the fears that used to be attached to African Americans "went underground and re-emerged to be applied not to blacks, but to aliens." Williamson reads the persecution of Leo Frank, then, as a double displacement, a mapping of old anxieties about African American sexuality onto a meek Jewish accountant who is meant to represent all foreignness (Williamson 222–23, 468, 471). But linear models of projection (*first this, then that*) will not do: the murder of Mary Phagan motivated a complex of worries that *never* could have been suitably addressed by a Black rapist: modernization, family dissolution, foreign influence in the South, and the possible collusion of Jew and African American for the benefit of Jews could not be explained by conjuring up the usual scapegoat, the "bestial" African American.

No matter whether Mary Phagan chose to continue working at the factory even after her stepfather requested that she stop, "Mary Phagan" easily came to serve as a symbol for "exploited working girl" (Kean 14). In fact, the inability of Phagan's parents to keep her at home might indeed be understood as further proof that industrialization was causing the breakdown of familial — which is to say patriarchal — power. It is worth recalling that intense fears about the sexual aspect of "girls" working in mills and factories stretch back at least to the middle of the nineteenth century; as Michael Denning notes, it became a commonplace in these times to wonder whether a female worker could possibly remain a virgin (190–91). The public obsession with Phagan's "virtue" then, reflected both a new worry and an old habit: if it was something like reflex to fret over the chastity of young working women, the conspicuous presence of Leo Frank in the showcase city of the New South raised novel anxieties about racial intermixture in a situation that was characterized by the power that the Jew held over southern whites and African Americans. Here then was motivation for those who would search to define the crime as something like rape — that heinous but relatively familiar crime — still somehow even worse for its foreign quality, its manifest unnaturalness, its intimations of reckless, uncontrolled modernity.

In an attempt to head off claims that Frank, as a Jew, was particularly likely to have committed the mysterious crime against Mary Phagan's body, Rabbi Stephen Wise contributed his opinion to a Jewish paper in Cleveland. Wise, a leading Zionist and rabbi for New York's Free Synagogue, was also an early participant in the National Association for the Advancement of Colored People (Diner 122–23). Relying on questionable data in his attempt to clear Frank, Wise admitted that Jews have "imperfections and failings" but insisted "crimes against women are not typical of our race" (qtd. in *Jewish Independent,* 28 May 1915: 8).[26] Although this is a fairly unremarkable and rote response for a religious leader to make on the occasion of a calamity befalling one of the people he represents, it is noteworthy for its acceptance of the racial terms of the case against Frank. What was to be gained by developing a racial (as opposed to social or religious) Jewish identity for Frank? No doubt his supporters, such as Rabbi Wise, believed that to pit Jewishness against its unacknowledged but real opponent — Blackness — could only redound positively to Frank. Establishing the moral meanings of Frank's Jewishness worked mostly to emphasize his non-Blackness. This, presumably, closed off the possibility of Frank having motivation in the heinous sexual assault on Mary Phagan. "Negro" serves here as the antithetical term in an implied construct, a formation that momentarily underscores Frank's divergence from normative whiteness, even as it plots the Jew as socially ready to take on those privileges conferred by whiteness. The Frank affair is shot through with similar racial calculations: Rabbi Wise implicitly presents a scheme in which he grants that Jews have their own particular *racial* "imperfections and failings" but still situates them on a vertical path up to whiteness.

I dwell on this example first because it is striking to find this sort of reasoning coming even from a racial liberal such as Rabbi Wise. But even more significantly, this example taken from an early supporter of the NAACP discloses that any "alliance" of African Americans and Jews that existed in the moment of the Leo Frank affair (and I would argue, at most times) has to be understood as primarily a rhetorical one: members of each group agree to use the other as a reliable reference point as they attempt to reorient their place in the world of American racial politics. To use a popular term of the era, Jews and African Americans exploited each other in the interests of "uplift." But group uplift often necessitated a handy negative comparison. Rabbi Wise's contributions to the NAACP need not be obscured by the fact that he also advanced exclusively Jewish interests, at times at the expense of African Americans.

And, of course, others, outside of the two groups, were more than happy to capitalize on the general sanction of racial interpretive categories. The most ardent supporters of a racial explanation for the crime were demagogue Tom Watson and, more subtly, Solicitor-General Hugh Dorsey. Leonard Dinnerstein has written that the "newspapers never clearly explained what was considered perverse about Frank, and the word meant different things to different people" (19). Dorsey took advantage of this ambiguity, implying through direct questioning of witnesses that Frank might be a few different kinds of pervert. Dorsey brought all of his insinuations together with one pointed literary analogy. To leave the jury with a strong (if still undefined) image of Frank as a Dr. Jekyll and Mr. Hyde split personality, Dorsey summoned the memory of Oscar Wilde. "Not even Oscar Wilde's wife," he told the jury, "suspected that he was guilty of such immoral practices." In case the jury did not immediately get his point, Dorsey reminded them that Wilde had "led the aesthetic movement; he was a scholar, a literary man, cool, calm and cultured." Even so, as Dorsey related, Wilde "went tottering to the grave, a confessed pervert" (Dorsey 31).

But Dorsey did not leave the implied comparison of the over-refined Jew and the "natural" African American unstated. He told the jury in almost the next breath that the "ignorant, like Jim Conley" only commit "the small crime" and do not know "anything about some of this higher type of crime." Bringing the argument all the way home, Dorsey concluded with poor syntax but wonderful directness that "a man of high intellect and wonderful endowments, which, if directed in the right line bring honor and glory, if those same faculties and talents are perverted and not controlled, as was the case with this man, they will carry him down" (Dorsey 32). Damned by success! The ultimate message embedded in Dorsey's comparison of Conley and Frank is that neither man was equipped for full citizenship, Conley because he was too ignorant, and Frank because he had become degraded through privilege and license.

Inspired by his need to have Conley and Frank function as competitors in this trial, Dorsey hit on a central axiom of Black-Jewish relatedness: he discovered that the surest way to create social distance between African Americans and Jews is to call attention to the differential elements of class status that lurk within their functionally related racial identities.[27] These constituents of class need not be directly expressed; indeed they often are revealed exclusively as matters of personal taste, style, and affect. In the Frank case the most available marker of class was sexuality, and Dorsey and others seized on the sexual aspects of the case to underscore why Frank was the correct villain; whether Frank was a voyeur, homosexual, or oral fetishist, it was clear that he had been contaminated by wealth and power. It was only left to Dorsey to finish the equation by calling attention to the unspoiled, primitive nature of Conley's sexuality. The fascinating thing about Dorsey's particular sleight-of-hand is that even as he drove a wedge between these two men, one Jewish and one African American, he managed simultaneously to insinuate that the groups represented by each man do belong together: in the racial landscape sketched by Dorsey, Jews and African Americans live together on the margins—denied a better social position by their "abnormal" sexuality.

Tom Watson's handling of the same general material was less subtle than Dorsey's had been. To begin, his interpretation of the two murder notes found by Mary Phagan's body focused on the phrase "play with" as it appeared in the first murder note ("i wright while play with me"). Though never explaining what he thought "play with" meant exactly, Watson found in this phrase proof that it could not have originated in the mind of an African American.

Watson wrote that "play with" suggested that "the tall, slim, black negro had had *unnatural* connection with the girl" and concluded that Frank must then be the villain, for this was "a vice not of robust negroes, but of decadent white men." Employing the same dichotomized thinking as Dorsey, Watson went on to write that "sodomy is not the crime of nature, barbarism or of lustful black brutes; it is the over-ripe fruit of civilization and is always indicative of a decaying society" (*Watson's Magazine*, Oct. 1915: 330).[28] Watson points to Frank's crime without defining it; Frank's sexuality, in this formulation, remains obscure but decidedly dangerous.[29] With the sexual comparison of Frank and Conley, Watson implicitly positioned himself on the same healthy (if beleaguered) middle ground that Dorsey staked out, pointing on one side to "overripe" Jews, and on the other to under-done African Americans. This crime, he made clear, belonged on the side of surfeit, not deficit, and thus Frank was the man.

Taking this "Sodomite Jew" as his text, Watson explicated for his presumably innocent readers what "pervert" meant, drawing a picture of a man who "stops at nothing," who might "crave boys, men, and even animals." Who, for Watson, fit this bill? Certainly not Jim Conley, whose "picture ... shows him to be a typical African negro, a perfect specimen of the human animal, just such a man as goes after black women *naturally*" (*Jeffersonian*, 5 Aug. 1915: 3). With his emphasis on Conley as a "typical African negro" I suspect that Watson was attempting to convince his readers that Conley was a "pureblooded" Negro, as opposed to the always-feared racially mixed people (like Jews?) who haunted the southern imagination as worst-case scenario even as they constituted a significant portion of the population. And this notwithstanding the frequent contemporaneous references to Conley as "ginger-colored" (Dinnerstein 21).

Having cleared the "robust and *natural*" Conley, Watson turned his attention back to Frank. This "vice of Sodom," of "civilization," could easily be attributed to the Jew, whose *"face look[ed] the part to perfection"* (*Watson's Magazine*, Aug. 1915: 219; emphasis in original). I have already recited the litany of anti-Semitic images attached to Frank's appearance; suffice to say, Watson trusted his readers to make the leap from foreign-looking to foreign-acting. Watson rendered his charges vaguely and wisely: by not specifying just what crimes he was imputing to Frank he could indict the Jewish man more broadly.

Usually Watson's attacks fixed on the image of Frank as the ravenous capitalist: Watson made specific mention of the testimony of one "fallen" factory girl who told "Judge Roan that she had a scar, on the tenderest part of her thigh, made by the teeth of Leo Frank" (*Jeffersonian*, 5 Aug. 1915: 3; see also *Watson's Magazine*, Aug. 1915: 200). Similarly, when Watson recounted that one factory worker "swore that Frank had proposed sodomy to her" we can assume the reference is understood to be to oral sex (*Watson's Magazine*, Oct. 1915: 316). Watson, we see, was particularly fond of imagery that brought to mind the picture of Jews as parasites. Other newspapers picked up on this thread, most notably the *Griffin (Georgia) News and Sun*, which summarized the crime by quoting approvingly from a Louisiana newspaper as follows: "Leo Frank belonged to that nameless class of degenerates who set aside the laws of nature herself. The medical examination and the marks on the girl's body showed that the crime was of a nature never known to have been perpetrated by a black man. The negro commits rape. His passions are bestial, but the crime committed against Mary Phagan is not known to the primal instincts of the elemental races of man. The Leo Franks are developed only in the higher states of civilization, never among even the laboring classes."[30]

This last phrase forges the direct link between Frank's perversion and his place in the employing class. The anxieties betrayed here are, as Nancy Mac-Lean has demonstrated, rooted in concern over who would control the bodies of "working girls" in the industrializing South. But I would add to this insight to note that what was particularly compelling about Leo Frank was that he raised a new worry over *how* the bodies of these "working girls" would be managed. Frank's power over these young women most obviously contributed to the sense that Jewish industrialists were threatening the patriarchal sanctity of the nuclear family in the New South; the public image of his sexual perversion also suggested that the young women under his supervision were at risk of being coerced to leave decency behind altogether.

Frank's presence posed two other dangers, as Watson saw things. First of all, whatever the specifics of Frank's sexuality, the organized defense of the Jew was setting a bad example for African Americans. Watson's fear was that if "every young negro buck should get the idea in his head that his race would place its secret societies behind him—as the Jews did for Frank...no white woman would be safe!" (*Jeffersonian*, 5 Aug. 1915: 4). Here the popular rhetoric that historically linked African Americans and Jews in a student/teacher relationship (Jews can show African Americans how to be as successful as they have been in America) is stripped bare: in Watson's fevered fantasy the real lesson Jews will teach African Americans is how to gain access to white women with no penalty.

The final and perhaps most frightening menace posed by Frank was derived from the vagueness of the term "sodomy," which was rarely explicitly defined; Watson noted that it could refer to sex with "boys, men, and even animals." Frank (and all Jew perverts) could presumably threaten southern men not only vicariously, by appropriating their women, but also more directly. In late July of 1915, Frank was attacked at the Milledgeville State Prison Farm by another prisoner, William Creen, who slashed Frank's throat and nearly killed him. According to one report the knife used by Creen was usually used for quartering pork in the prison kitchen: "What subtle irony in the choice of such a weapon with which to inflict death upon one of Abraham's seed!" (Knight 1185).[31] Creen told the new governor, Nathaniel Harris, that he "had been called 'from on high' to murder the Jew, and...had tried to kill Frank to prevent other prisoners from being harmed, should an attempt be made to storm the prison and abduct" Frank (qtd. in Dinnerstein 138). Logical enough reasoning, but Tom Watson uncovered, and highlighted a much more shocking explanation: rumor had it that "Creen told Governor Harris he cut Frank because Frank had tried to sodomize him" (*Jeffersonian*, 5 Aug. 1915: 3). Added to the deep concern about the loss of patriarchal control over working girls and women, Watson finally revealed the fear that previously had dared not speak its name: after satisfying his desires with southern white girls, the Jewish capitalist was now turning his perverted attention to the men of the South.

The accusation that Frank performed cunnilingus on southern white women, as I will soon discuss, certainly contained at least a hint that Frank was homosexual. Rene Girard has explained that a significant part of the "sacrificial crisis" (the social chaos that requires that a symbolic victim be located and punished) is the feminization of men; the violence done to the sacrifice helps reinstate appropriate gender symmetry to the community (*Violence and the Sacred* 141). If we recall that the one unquestionable "assault" made by Leo Frank was an economic one—he took over control of a southern pencil factory and enjoyed the associated benefits—it becomes possible to understand how Frank's supposed assault on Mary Phagan could ultimately be translated as homosexual rape. Frank's direct control over Mary Phagan and Jim Conley was frightening enough, but the most daunting aspect of the Jewish man's power was the visible way it displaced southern white men: hence the body of Mary Phagan was left behind as the complex competition of anxieties raised by her murder finally surfaced in the accusation that Frank was trying to sodomize other men.

Sundry and often contradictory claims about Frank's sexuality were made before, during, and after his trial, but I want to turn now to the central sexual charge made at the trial—that Leo Frank was, perhaps of necessity, obsessed with oral sex. In studying sexual acts in history (or even claims about sexual acts) it is important not to imagine that what is in question is the meaning of individual interactions. While each sexual act has its own logic and meaning (maybe only to the participants), there is a huge difference between those acts and the larger social question of how these acts are publicized, interpreted, and placed into context. Robert Padgug has explained that no histories of sexuality should focus only on "acts"; even discrete expressions of sexuality are shot through with signs of the "active social relations" that produce them (22).

The usefulness of Jim Conley's testimony on Leo Frank's perversion, whether it was coached or not and whether it was true or not, depended on whether cunnilingus could actively carry a variety of messages about the terrible things going on in the National Pencil Company factory. The many *stories* told by the attribution of such perverse behavior to Frank might lack coherence—indeed, they might contradict one another—but taken together they helped mark off Frank's difference not only from Conley but from the standards of white manhood as well. Conley was himself authorized to articulate the central sexual charges against Frank because his own sexual persona— conveyed by the color of his skin and his appropriate speech acts—was easily fathomed: it was clearly unlike that attributed to Frank and could be incorporated into a workable vision of southern life.

In his fifth affidavit and during the trial Jim Conley claimed that he had often served in the past as lookout in the factory while Frank held sexual assignations. This line of testimony led to the conclusion that Frank had killed Mary Phagan in anger, perhaps accidentally, after she refused his advances. I now want to quote at some length Conley's statements about what happened on the day of the murder.

> Mr. Frank was standing up there at the top of the steps and shivering and trembling and rubbing his hands like this. His eyes were large and they looked right funny. . . . After I got to the top of the steps, he asked me, "Did you see that little girl who passed here just a while ago?" and I told him I saw one come along there and she come back again, and then I saw another one come along there and she hasn't come back down, and he says, "Well, that one you say didn't come back down, she came into my office and I went back there to see if the little girl's work had come, and I wanted to be with the little girl, and she refused me, and I struck her and I guess I struck her too hard and she fell and hit her head against something, and I don't know how bad she got hurt. Of course you know I ain't built like other men." The reason he said that was I had seen him in a position I haven't seen any other man that has got children. I have seen him in the office two or three times before Thanksgiving and a lady was in his office, and she was sitting down in a chair (and she had her clothes up to here, and he was down on his knees, and she had her hands on Mr. Frank. I have seen him another time there in the packing room with a young lady lying on the table, she was on the edge of the table when I saw her). (*Brief of Evidence* at 55; see also Dinnerstein 41)

The introduction of Frank's specific perversion reads, of course, as a non sequitur in Conley's testimony. Additionally, Conley's suggestion, if taken literally, is that he had previously seen other men in this position and knew that they were in it because of a defect, and not as a matter of sexual choice. Frank and his wife had no children, a fact that provided some circumstantial support for Conley's depiction of a nonprocreative act at the core of Frank's sexuality.[32]

Perhaps most immediately striking is the way that Conley offered his listeners the opportunity to become voyeurs. Conley's story compelled the jury and the general public to *watch* him *watch* Frank do something perverse to southern white women. Conley's testimony afforded some pleasures for anti-Frank partisans — his testimony at least offered grounds for condemning Frank — but these pleasures were surely complicated by the specific contents of the spectacle he described.

Frank's attorneys did all they could to break Conley's testimony. After their failure to discredit him, they attempted to have the information about Frank's earlier sexual practices struck from the record, as irrelevant to the present trial (Dinnerstein 46).[33] In addition, according to one student of the case, "on several occasions during the trial, even Frank's attorneys seemed to accept implicitly that their client may not always have been a model of propriety in sexual matters" (Dinnerstein 174; see also Lindemann 256). All of this helped add to the image of Frank as a pervert, as did the testimony from a variety of other witnesses.

But what possible meanings might have been attached to Conley's description of cunnilingus? What meanings might this postulated sexual act possibly carry? It should first be noted that one has to look long and hard to find *any* substantial allusions to cunnilingus in the United States in this era. A number of women blues singers advocated the pleasures of cunnilingus in the 1920s and beyond — perhaps none so colorfully as Maggie Jones in her "Anybody Here Want to Try My Cabbage?" (1924).[34] Professional sexologists, on the other hand, were less celebratory of this particular act: one 1899 sex manual suggested that cunnilingus was exhausting to women and could even kill them (Bullough 547). Havelock Ellis (something of a progressive) wrote in 1905 that he considered cunnilingus to be an acceptable lead-up to "tumescence" but thought it a perversion if it became the sole activity of the sexual encounter (Ellis 19–20).

Moving beyond the pure mechanics of cunnilingus, its central role as a provider of cultural meaning was as a clear marker of difference. Typical here was the Russian doctor at the turn of the century who referred to cunnilingus as "sapphism" and insisted that it was never practiced in Russia; more recent commentators on the history of sexuality have noted that cunnilingus has frequently been interpreted as "somehow a homosexual act" (Engelstein 188; Gagnon and Simon 202). For his part, Havelock Ellis was certainly conscious of how discussions of cunnilingus often incorporated broader attempts at marking off social distance: just as the Greeks once considered cunnilingus to be a Phoenician practice, "it is now commonly considered French" (Ellis 21).[35] The practice of cunnilingus, insofar as it circulated as a social image at all, also likely contained strong suggestions of upper-class decadence (Birken 50–51; Kinsey, Pomeroy, and Martin 576).

It is crucial to notice that in the Frank case the focal point of this Jewish man's sexuality is not his genitals but his mouth. In *Black Skin, White Masks,* Frantz Fanon writes: "In relation to the Negro, everything takes place on the genital level.... The Jew is feared because of his potential for acquisitiveness. 'They' are everywhere. The banks, the stock exchanges, the government are infested with 'them.' 'They' control everything.... As for the Negroes, they have tremendous sexual powers.... The government and the civil service are at the mercy of the Jews. Our women are at the mercy of the Negroes" (157). Fanon's sweeping comparison of Blacks and Jews is of course too broad to apply to every experience. But his central insight is worth holding on to: the danger of Frank's Jewishness was never described as a recognizable sexual threat. While Fanon went on to suggest that Jews are never feared *because* of their bodies, it would be appropriate in Frank's case to argue that the Jewish man was attacked not because he lacked sexuality altogether but because his sexuality seemed unhealthy: it is partial, unwhole, nongenital.

What did it mean for Conley (perhaps having been coached) to say that Frank admitted that he was not built like other men? Governor John Slaton, one of the more discerning commentators on the case, was vocal in his skepticism about the perversion charges. He wondered where Conley might have come up with such a suggestion and in his commutation order recounted the explanation offered by one of Frank's lawyers that "someone may have made him [Conley] the suggestion because Jews were circumcised." During the commutation hearing Frank's representative said of the perversion charge that "whoever suggested it undertook to graft it on to the very common-place idea that as a Jew he had been circumcised, and he was in that respect 'unlike other men' in the eyes and mind of a negro like Conley." This lawyer went on to suggest that this explanation would satisfy Conley because the brain "of the negro ordinarily is equal to a creek eel."[36] (In fact, Frank was exam-

ined by physicians before his original trial and was certified by them to be
sexually normal. As if you can tell by looking [Busch 57]. We are left to wonder what the doctors were looking for and what they found.)

Slaton made another subtle comment on the sexual issues of the case in this
commutation order when he wrote, with a sly wink for those looking closely,
that "there is every probability that the virtue of Mary Phagan was not lost
on the 26th of April" (qtd. in Kean 202; see also MacLean 918). Of course
Slaton might simply have meant that Phagan was not sexually assaulted, but
in the context of the governor's numerous reservations in the case it seems at
least possible that he was claiming that her "virtue" had been lost previously.[37] So, while Slaton left the door open to the oral sex charge (which, it
should be mentioned, was also a capital crime in Georgia at the time), he also
undercut the assumptions of purity that had surrounded Phagan since her
death (Lindemann 256).

More significant, however, was the connection Jim Conley forged between
Frank's Jewishness — represented for now by his circumcised penis — and his
incapacity or unwillingness to perform like "other" men. This charge, as Frank's
lawyer and Governor Slaton noted, was hardly unprecedented. Gilman has
written extensively on the various cultural meanings carried by the image of
circumcision in modern European culture; sometimes confused or linked with
castration, circumcision emphasizes the weakness — that is, the feminization —
of the Jewish man (*Freud* 49–92). But circumcision also implies the danger
that Jews represent, for a number of reasons. First, if Jews are willing to cut
flesh off their own penises, there is no telling what they might do to non-Jews;
also various images of disease surrounded circumcision, many of which derived
from the notion that the circumciser spread syphilis through the Jewish community and beyond through the action of putting his mouth to the cut baby's
penis to suck the blood (Gilman, *Jew's Body* 93–99). Gilman summarizes this
whole cycle of reasoning nicely, suggesting that it "is the Aryan who suffers
from the trauma of the Jew's circumcision" (*Freud* 91). The construction of
Frank at the trial, in the press, and in letters written at the time was of a man
dangerous not in a genital sense (as the South's favorite rape suspect usually
was), but in a far stranger, less completely understood manner.

There was only one major exception to the trend to see Frank as threatening in a nongenital yet still sexual way. This came with the response of the Georgia Supreme Court to an appeal for a new trial that Frank made in the autumn of 1913. Frank's major claim in this appeal was that Conley's testimony as to his perversion should have been ruled inadmissible. The court decided that it was acceptable for Conley to relate that Frank was not "built like other men" because it offered a motive for Frank and made Conley's presence as a lookout more believable. The court defended its decision with the following analogy: "Suppose on the trial of one accused of murder it should be sought to show that the accused was armed with a deadly weapon, and a witness should testify that the accused said to him about the time of the homicide, 'You know what I always carry in my pocket.' Would there be any doubt that the witness would be allowed to testify that the accused had previously informed him that he always carried a pistol, or had on previous occasions exhibited to him a pistol in his pocket?"[38]

With this remarkable rhetorical leap, the highest court of Georgia rewrote Frank's condition. No longer was his special status to be characterized as a deficiency ("not built like other men"); instead Frank's penis now stands as a loaded gun! Aside from this passage, however, even this court stuck to images that depicted Frank as a consumer of young women. The court refuted the contention made by Frank's lawyers that even if lascivious behavior with other women was proved, no intent toward Mary Phagan would have been established; this, the court argued, put "too narrow a construction upon subject of motive and plan." The opinion held: "If a man should construct a pit with the general purpose of catching the ewe lambs of his neighbors, it would be trivial to say that, if charged with catching a certain one, he did not have that particular lamb in view when he dug the pit."[39] Thus, the Georgia State Supreme Court recast this slight, nervous accountant as a dangerous wolf.[40]

Apart from this major exception the tendency was to follow Conley's hint and consider Frank's sexuality to be found in his face: hence the numerous references to his odd looks, especially his lips and eyes. The attention paid to Frank's mouth is particularly important and might offer further insight into the possible meanings attached to the cunnilingus charge. As I have argued, the claim that Frank was not built like other men obviously feminized him; the associated charge that he performed cunnilingus on women opens up the question of who is the active (male) player in such a sexual act. To put it most bluntly, it is not altogether clear from Conley's description who is doing what to whom: recall his depiction of Frank "down on his knees" with a woman who "had her hands on Mr. Frank." In one possible reading of the cunnilingus charge, then, we find Frank on his knees, becoming the passive partner — the "done to" rather than the "doer." (And certainly the Georgia Supreme Court's invention of a "pit" to describe Frank holds the implication that this legal body was effeminizing Frank.[41]) Male passivity, as Jonathan Dollimore remarks, is very commonly interpreted as an abdication of power, and in this case Frank surrendered not only his racial responsibilities (letting Conley watch all of this) but also those of his gender. Frank is not only implicated in the break-down of familial patriarchal control in his role as an employer of young women, but once these workers are in his control he does not even exploit them in a recognizably (and acceptably) masculine way (263–64).

Jews were rendered suspect in Atlanta by their willingness to interact with African Americans in ways that transgressed the established southern codes of racial interaction. Frank is placed even further outside the pale of proper behavior for a white man through this image of his submissive sexuality. It is interesting to note in this context that in his novel, which draws heavily on the Frank case, Richard Kluger bravely contemplated the possibility that the perversion charges had some basis in fact, but still invested the Leo Frank character with the social and sexual power that was stripped from him in the original case; in Kluger's version the factory manager's perversion is condensed in the image of a working woman (a stenographer) kneeling in front of him to perform fellatio (333).

A number of recent commentators have made clear how Jewish men, through their perceived physical and mental weakness, have been likened to women (Garber 78, 224–25; Gilman, *Jew's Body* 63–64). It is possible to read Jim Conley's testimony on Leo Frank's sexuality as a cooperative attempt to portray the Jewish man as effeminate. Again, regardless of where Conley's charge came from, what really matters is how it came to find such a receptive audience. Following this line, it is worth taking note of Rene Girard's contention that in major times of crisis, sacrificial victims who are chosen to re-store order must "bear a certain resemblance to the object they replace" (*Violence* 11). The sexual violence done to Mary Phagan was enigmatic, implying as it did the use of mouth and/or hands where a penis was expected. This, in turn, suggested perversion in general, and cunnilingus more specifically, all of which placed the masculinity of the perpetrator in question. Fixing on the Jewish man and creating an aura of effeminacy around him turned Leo Frank into something like that which he allegedly destroyed himself. The prosecution and lynching of Frank, then, allowed for a symbolic reenactment of the murder of Mary Phagan, and one that would have been much harder to construct with Jim Conley as designated villain: turning a Jewish man into a woman (especially in Georgia in 1913) was more easily accomplished than doing the same to an African American man, who would have associated with him all the customary signs of hypermasculinity. Even the lynching of Frank brought him into closer proximity with Phagan: Frank's killers originally planned to hang him right near Mary Phagan's gravesite but settled for a spot outside of her hometown when they realized they were running short of time (Dinnerstein 140).

The picture of Frank performing cunnilingus on Southern white women signified, in part, that Frank had a diffuse and unstable sexuality. This exposed Frank as being too much like a woman — too weak, that is — to be trusted to exercise properly the authority entrusted to him as factory superintendent. At the same time, however, the specific form of this perversion charge was the logical condensation of a competing belief that Frank was all-powerful, completely able to exert his will over the factory population. We should not be troubled by the paradox implied here; as a Jewish capitalist Frank's public persona was overdetermined by imagery that would draw him as physically weak but socially strong. Daniel T. Rodgers has noted that capitalists in this era were commonly depicted as embodying a confusing array of characteristics, "a mixture of indolence and shrewdness, sloth and ambition" (211). The capitalist, like the Jew, was "corrupter, thief, and parasite" — in short, physically debased but still able to accrue power from the hard work of others. It is also worth noting, as historian Gail Bederman has, that the early years of the century were marked by a recognizable crisis in masculinity owing to less self-employment, labor unrest, and the women's movement, among other factors. For many social leaders of the time it became important for white men to demonstrate both the power of their bodies *and* "the racial ability to restrain . . . the masculine powers" (Bederman 12–14, 84).

Recalling all the attention that was paid to Frank's mouth during and after his trial, it seems reasonable to consider the cunnilingus charge in its most concrete aspect. Evidence that Frank had his mouth on southern women, that he had actually bitten some, insinuates that the Jewish capitalist had the inclination and the power to consume southern working women. With this in mind, I want to conclude this section with a final consideration of the messages carried by the image of Frank on his knees in front of a southern woman with her skirt hiked up. One of the prerequisites of civilization, as Freud put it, is that all of the partial sexual instincts must submit to the primacy of genitality (95, 107–12). Freud explains this by pointing to the social need for sexuality to be channeled toward propagating the race. As such, the partial sex instincts (what he called "polymorphous perversity") have to be tabooed as perversions (87–88). Freud's insights were extended later by Herbert Marcuse, who suggested that the ban on polymorphous perversity is necessary to capitalism because it forces workers to focus their sexuality in one place (their genitals) leaving everything else free for work (41, 44).

What kind of man could take time out from work in a factory to perform oral sex on women? It must be a man who has freedom both temporally (he is not on the time clock) and spatially (he does not need to concentrate his sexuality in his genitals alone because he does not need the rest of his body for his labor). The image is almost too perfect: the capitalist, blessed with the leisure to be polymorphously perverse, along with so many other things, devours even the one part of a working woman that is supposed to be reserved for her private sexual (genital) life. Frank's perversion distinguished him specifically as a capitalist, living off the work of others, and in this Frank might have been perceived as a conspicuous consumer of the worst kind; if this image of oral sex communicates anything, it is that the Jewish factory owner is nonproductive (and also nonreproductive).[42] The equation, then, stands as Jew = capitalist = pervert = parasite. This was not the first time that a Jew would be damned for his nonproductive place in the societal order.[43] The cunnilingus charge laid bare the mechanics of bodily exploitation necessary to the healthy workings of capitalism; as Richard Dyer writes, "much of the cultural history of the past few centuries has been concerned with finding ways of making sense of the body, while disguising the fact that its predominant use has been as the labor of the majority in the interests of the few" (138). Frank's crime, then, revealed itself locally in the sexual abuse and murder of Mary Phagan, and more generally with his ostentatious flaunting of capitalist privilege.

The factory, even in a booster city like Atlanta, had long been condemned as a place for the promiscuous social mixing of class, race, and gender. The industrial workplace does not necessitate the prohibition of all sexuality, but it does demand that sexuality be surveyed and controlled by the owner or manager. In Conley's version of events, the power of the capitalist—usually hidden in the mist of delegated authority—is brought to stark visibility. Frank's power is immense if dispersed: he can force women to accept whatever kind of sexual advances he wants to make and can even compel Jim Conley to watch. In this respect it is tempting to think of Jim Conley's testimony as a descendant of the captivity narrative—a tried-and-true formula for integrating numerous social anxieties into a linear account of the sexual threat posed by racial outsiders; in the captivity narratives of the seventeenth and eighteenth centuries white women were constantly being kidnapped by wild Indians. The factory was Atlanta's new frontier.

What was most striking about the Frank case was how directly it coded the dangers of the factory system in a compact sexual image. Thomas Laquer has written of how the sexual body "haunts society and reminds it of its fragility" (214); Jim Conley's dramatization of Leo Frank's perversion reminded southern white men that once "their" women went off to the factory anything could happen. The prosecution responded to this chaos by enlisting the power of Jim Conley—his natural-seeming sexuality and his closeness to Frank—in order to convict the Jew.

The perversion charge depicted Leo Frank as the enveloping Other, come South to exploit women. Joined to this invention was the popular image of the Jewish man as purveyor of vice (with particular attention to the needs of African American men). In the decades to come, the notion that Jews often contaminated white purity by proxy would circulate; Adolf Hitler, for instance, believed that Jews stage-managed the deployment of Black troops along the Rhine during the World War I era as a conscious insult and threat to the German people (325, 624).

One irate letter writer responding to Frank's commutation related feeling dumbfounded when he read in the paper that Slaton had "commuted the sentence of that moral degenerate + whoremonger Frank."[44] How would an observer of this case decide that, among other things, Frank was a "whoremonger"? There were claims during the trial that Frank had frequently visited a house of ill repute and had tried to reserve a room there on the day Mary Phagan was killed, but this would make Frank a "john" and not a pimp. Charges also arose during the trial that Frank ran an informal prostitution ring in the basement of the National Pencil Company factory, or at least winked at its operation (*Brief of Evidence* at 50). At least one witness at Frank's original trial claimed that a sofa was kept in the basement of the factory to be used for immoral purposes (Cahan 418–19); these charges were floated in Atlanta newspapers as soon as Frank became a suspect (Golden 44).

There are a number of less concrete ways that this construction of Jewish capitalist-as-pimp might have functioned. First, we should recall here that for a white woman to be "forced" to work in a factory was widely thought to be akin to becoming a prostitute. If these women were reduced to the status of prostitutes, it is obvious who was supervising their work. The terms of this syllogism itself underscore the more general point that industrialization caused a shift in the negotiation of sexual identities and practices from the family to the public sphere (D'Emilio and Freedman 166–67).

Even more pointedly, pimping had a special resonance as a charge lodged against Jewish men in this era: from approximately 1911 to 1914, a worldwide "white slavery" panic took hold, a major constituent of which was the contention that Jewish men were overrepresented in the prostitution business as pimps and procurers (called "cadets") in America.[45] According to one report, at least one billion pages of print had been expended on the subject by 1912 in the United States alone (Bristow 41; see also Cordasco 32). From Warsaw and Odessa to Buenos Aires and New York, tales of abduction of innocent young women by evil Jews were disseminated in this era. Official pronouncements, quasi-pornographic novels and plays, and commissioned studies all contributed to a sense that the problem of white slavery had intensified in these years. A villain in the most popular white slavery novel of all, Reginald Kauffman's *The House of Bondage* (1910), is described in terms similar to those applied to Frank during the trial: a "member of the persistent race," this man has thick lips and a "gray glance" which has "a penetrating calculation about it" (19).

The drama of Phagan's murder fit quite explicitly into one of the major paradigms for white slave procurement as outlined by reformer Jane Addams. Addams explained in a book on white slavery that young working women were particularly vulnerable to seduction during slack seasons in the labor calendar, when they might be more easily coerced to accept any available work. Although Mary Phagan had not been permanently released from the factory, she had not worked most of the week because a shipment of brass fasteners for erasers had not come in on time. As a result, Phagan had been forced to make a special trip to the factory on Saturday to collect her pay of $1.20 for one ten-hour day (Addams 85; see also Golden 10; Dinnerstein 71). Just a few days after her murder, the *Atlanta Constitution* reported that Mary Phagan had been "the victim of a white slavery plot that was foiled only by her murder" (29 Apr. 1913: 2). In this version of events, Phagan was nearly lured into a white slavery ring but escaped only through her death.

In the United States, an interest in the special criminality of Jews had been circulating since before the turn of the century. The Lexow and Mazet investigations of 1894 and 1899 both exposed the elaborate connections linking Tammany Hall and the police with Jews and criminal activity (Goren 134–35). Many historians agree, however, that it was in the years just preceding World War I that Jewish vice became a subject of primary interest in the United States. Brief mention of two exemplary moments, one in 1908 and the other in 1912 might usefully bracket the period of most profound concern about Jewish crime. Theodore Bingham, police commissioner of New York City, published an article in 1908 in *North American Review* that argued that 50 percent of New York's criminals were "Hebrews." The article received wide play in the New York press, and although Bingham's numbers were off and he finally retracted the statement, his pronouncement offered a crystallized image of the special penchant Jews had for illegal activity (Bingham 383; see also Goren 34–35).

The real high point for discussions of Jewish criminality came a bit later, however, with the murder of Herman "Rosy" Rosenthal, a New York gambler who had turned states' evidence. After implicating a policeman who was involved with a major vice ring, Rosenthal was gunned down in public; the entire cast of characters in this scandal, with a few exceptions, was made up of Jews (Goren 136; Feingold 141). Solicitor-General Hugh Dorsey accessed this cluster of images surrounding Jews during his closing remarks at the trial by including a reference to the Jewish gangsters who killed Rosenthal within a litany of bad Jews he cited in order to prove that not all Jews were law-abiding citizens (Cahan 467; Golden 184).[46]

The white slavery panic intersected at numerous points with the general concern over Jewish villainy in American cities. Two articles written by George Kibbe Turner for *McClure's* (1909) provided abundant data on the subject. In "The Daughters of the Poor" and in "Tammany's Control of New York by Professional Criminals," Turner coupled the corruption of Tammany Hall with the proliferation of the Jewish pimp. This latter, as Turner put it, was "a product of New York politics, who has vitiated, more than any other single agency, the moral life of the great cities of America in the past ten years" (Turner, "Tammany's" 121). Detailing the very real operations of the white slavery network, Turner also gave voice to a rank anti-Semitism that he cloaked in the mantle of the Progressive reformer. Turner was not alone, however, and 1909 ended with a report from the Dillingham Commission that also implicated Jews in the white slave trade (Goren 149). In response Jews from all over the world organized a conference in London in 1910 to discuss ways to combat this aspect of the "social evil."

Ruth Rosen helpfully summarizes some of the direct causes of the white slavery scare in America, noting that the very concept of white slavery served "to deflect attention away from the very real social and economic factors that led women into prostitution. The class guilt of middle-class Americans for conditions that gave rise to prostitution was projected onto a few villainous white slavers, typically represented as foreigners" (133). Producing a white slavery scare was one way, then, to open discussions of industrialization and modernization in general. This is not to deny, as Rosen herself makes clear, that an international system of compulsory prostitution had long been in effect. Instead, as Edward Bristow explains, the actual presence of a network of white slavery provided a convenient vocabulary for speaking about growing fears over the purity of the racial stock of a variety of national communities; an obsession with the Jewish presence in white slavery (a presence that was real enough, whatever its socioeconomic causation) dovetailed with the material of the blood libel, the charge first popularized in medieval times and reinvigorated in Europe toward the end of the nineteenth century. The blood-libel myth, like the white slavery accusation, depended on images of defenseless children being exploited by deviant Jewish men (Bristow 41–42, 107).[47] The idea that Leo Frank acted as a pimp refashioned this shaky analogy into a logical chain: already a white slaver in his role as factory manager, Frank then used Mary Phagan for his own immoral purposes, made her sexually available to the whole range of factory workers, and then killed her after satisfying his own particularly Jewish needs.

Perhaps even more damaging to Frank was a related implication of the pimping charge. Central to the state's case was Frank's perverse sexuality; the most damning testimony came from Jim Conley, who claimed to know what he knew because Frank had asked him to serve as lookout on numerous occasions while the Jewish man committed debaucheries in his office. Here again the white slave theme might have been accessed. Boys often served a sort of apprenticeship to pimps by acting as lookouts for them; later, according to Jane Addams, they would be promoted to more important positions (107). In this sense, then, it should be emphasized that on top of the horrors Frank was physically visiting on his victims, he was also opening the door for the gaze of the African American man to rest on the bodies of white women. If, as Conley testified, he had seen Mr. Frank kneeling before a woman who was "sitting down in a chair" with "her clothes up to here," then that means Conley saw the white woman with her clothes up to here. Added to Frank's actual bodily transgression, then, was the implied violence he allowed Conley to perform. One editorialist in Texas made this case blatantly, arguing that if Conley turned out to be the killer, Frank should be hanged anyway, "for having that kind of a negro working around a place where little girls were employed."[48] Jews and African Americans are bad enough taken separately; together their evil increases exponentially.

The description of Leo Frank as pimp can be even further complicated by returning to the specifics of Jim Conley's claim: according to Conley, Frank had numerous sexual assignations before April of 1913 and always used the janitor as a "lookout." One point to make about this situation is that regardless of the parade of women who figure as characters in this narrative, the only two regular participants in this serial activity are Conley and Frank. Conley and Frank, that is, are the couple who stand at the center of the history of factory sexuality described in the janitor's testimony: whatever Frank *does* Conley *sees*. A protest might be made that if my analysis is correct up until now, then it is Frank who serves as the object of Conley's gaze — that Frank in essence pimped *himself* for Conley, and the women involved represent only the justification for bringing the two men together. Indeed, as I have outlined, the specific development of Frank's perversity combined images of him as ravenously active and wretchedly passive. Within the indictment of Frank as pimp, therefore, it is possible to find the suggestion that the Jewish man was offering up his own body, along with the bodies of southern white women, to the transgressive gaze of the Black man. To imagine Frank in the position of the "done-to" as Conley watches is not, however, to connote Frank's total abjection. Quite to the contrary, Frank might be better understood in this tableau as flaunting the pleasures of his body in a labor setting. The Jewish white slave trader not only put his women workers on display but also found social opportunities to offer up the sight of his own *nonworking body* as an indication of his prestige.

George Kibbe Turner scornfully described the low-level cadet "with plastered hair, a pasty face, and most ingratiating manners" as a familiar site at Lower East Side dancehalls; here the cadet was procuring new bodies — at work in this sense — while also displaying his privileged position as one who lives off the labor of others ("Daughters" 56; see also Roe 94–95). Whatever the origin of the pimping motif, it symbolically granted great powers to Leo Frank even as it pounded another nail in his coffin. Abraham Cahan, in his retrospective account of the case, found it instructive that the walls of Frank's office were made of glass. No sensible man, Cahan assures his readers, would dare carry on such bizarre sexual activities in open view of all the factory's workers (420–21). But Cahan misses the main point here: essential to the rendering of Frank as perverse is the admission/allegation that he wielded such vast power in the factory that he could do as he pleased. In this instance, Frank's authority is demonstrated as he dares to arrange the spectacle of himself performing oral sex on a white woman as an African American man watches. To put it another way, the plausibility of all of Conley's accusations against Frank depend on the belief that within the factory Frank had begun to translate his palpable economic power into an elaborate regime of social control that contravened the basic principles of southern life.

Frank himself seemed to have understood how closely his social authority was wrapped up with his position at the National Pencil Company factory. Even though he was treated as a suspect from the very beginning of the investigation of Mary Phagan's murder, Frank first hired counsel and private detectives, as Leonard Dinnerstein put it, "to protect the National Pencil Factory's interests" (4, 6). Harry Golden adds that Frank "worried incessantly about the adverse publicity" surrounding his case and was "always crestfallen when he was told that his notoriety, as well as his absence, had indeed hurt business" (66).

I have been arguing that Leo Frank's alleged perversion was envisioned to be threatening in a number of ways. First, he was sexually aberrant and fed his disgusting appetites with defenseless southern working women, who, paradoxically, could also be understood to be penetrating Frank in a way that reversed traditionally gendered sexual roles. Second, he ignored all rules of societal conduct in allowing for at least symbolic race mixing in the National Pencil Company factory. This second possibility did not create the volume or volubility of responses that the first construct did; most commentators on the case assumed an either/or aspect to the case (Frank versus Conley) and could not or would not entertain the even more threatening chance that a both/and scenario had obtained. One letter writer from Chicago did suggest to Slaton that the "Negro + the Jew were both in this crime—both in the bldg [sic] when it was done," but few picked up on this strand.[49] This deserves scrutiny when we consider that Conley was in fact convicted as an accessory after the fact;

after all, Conley admitted carrying Mary Phagan's body to the basement of the National Pencil Company factory after Frank killed her. In this scenario—the "true" scenario according to Hugh Dorsey and the Frank jury—both Frank and Conley are intimate with the body of Mary Phagan, but some kind of overload apparently made it difficult to consider that the Jew and the African American were sexual outlaws together.

Even so, once the production of perversity was set in motion it was no longer possible to contain all of its meanings. But while Jim Conley's report was meant to purge Atlanta of all evil by projecting it onto Leo Frank, it had disturbing implications for any white men following the trial. Where, in Conley's scenario, does a white man stand? In Conley's film-worthy rendition of Leo Frank's perversion and the murder of Mary Phagan, there are no flesh-and-blood white male players; more troubling yet for a white man observing the trial (from the jury box, in the newspapers, and so on) is the lack of any satisfactory subject position in which he might imagine himself. With whom would a white man identify as Conley unveiled this picture of a (coerced) African American man watching a Jewish man perform cunnilingus on an (unwilling) southern woman? In Conley's frightful representation of the factory, not only did Frank *personally* lack a working penis but he also shrugged off the burden of phallic power. One way to measure the magnitude of the anxieties set off by the crimes against Mary Phagan is to take note of the fact that southern white men permitted—required really—the gaze of an African American man to structure the narrative of degraded factory life that would condemn Leo Frank. And Conley did not only relate this narrative of Jewish evil; according to Harry Golden, Conley amplified his spoken testimony on the witness stand by whipping back an imaginary skirt (122)! For white southern men one moral of this story was that within the factory system they were invisible, powerless, and obsolete. Frank's attorney Reuben Arnold thought he was scoring points when, on appeal, he emphasized the absurdity of Conley's "lookout" story: "What white man could this negro have kept out anyhow?" (Arnold 39). But as Mary Phagan's death proved, white men *were* being kept out of the factory long enough for a young white woman to be murdered there—most likely by either a Jewish man or an African American man.

The most difficult matter for all concerned with the case was how to describe the relationship of African American and Jew within it. While Hugh Dorsey needed Conley to describe his close relationship to Frank in convincing detail, he also had to be able to make clear that the motive force of this particular Black-Jewish relation was to be found in the power and perversion of the Jewish man who managed it. The frightful both/and that was built into the perversion charges was defused by the insistence that in the factory only Leo Frank was endowed with *agency*. One good reason to convict Frank, then, was to guarantee that he would no longer be able to stage indiscriminate mixing in the factory. Following the prosecution's lead, most interested Jews and African Americans insisted on establishing as much distance as possible between the two men; the circumstance of the murder notes made this especially difficult to do, since here the prosecution established a persuasive criminal link between African American and Jew. It was only after Frank's lynching that a major effort was made to stoke the engines of analogy and find more positive terms of comparison to bring Jew and African American back into a healthier rhetorical proximity.

"THE NIGHT WITCH
DID IT"

Narrating Villainy in the Frank Case

omparison of Leo Frank and Jim Conley as racial representatives was undertaken most frequently on a very general level: what kind of person could be responsible for all of this? The question that most contemporary commentators on the case wanted to answer was whether a Jew or an African American was more likely to have committed this crime. Again, the enormity of a conspiracy of equals was rarely suggested as an answer to the mystery, and the either/or construct was a first principle for those interested in the question only as a parlor game, and for those who were privately deciding which man to lynch. Underpinning the specifics of the Frank case, of course, was an unspoken but urgent need to ameliorate a generalized anxiety caused by the increasing public and uncontrolled visibility of racial outsiders: Jews and African Americans were certainly not newcomers to Atlanta, but it was only in the post-Reconstruction city that the two groups, separately and together, came to represent a deeply felt threat to white Atlanta (Williamson 429–44).

A major theme of the discussion around the Frank case is that African Americans and Jews could be understood as intimately related even as they participated in a life-and-death struggle against each other. One way to describe the competition of African American and Jew in this case is to take a careful look at the controversy surrounding the murder notes found near Mary Phagan's body. A weird and fervent discourse derived from the indeterminacy of the meaning of these notes; discussions surrounding the notes articulated the confused (but not random) state of affairs inspired by the murder of Mary Phagan.

Two murder notes, purportedly written by Mary Phagan, were found near her body in the National Pencil Company factory (Dinnerstein 3). They read:

> Mam that negro hire down here did this i went to make water and he push me down that hole a long tall negro black that hoo it wase long sleam tall negro i wright while play with me
> he said he wood love me land down play like the night witch did it but that long tall black negro did buy his slef.[1]

Because "night witch" would be read as "night watchman" immediate suspicion was directed at Newt Lee, recently hired for that position at the factory. According to a few accounts of the case, in fact, Lee volunteered that the locution "night witch" was a manifest attempt to pin blame on him (Golden 19).

But then Jim Conley's ability to write was discovered—a piece of information that Frank himself apparently provided (Dinnerstein 22). By the end of May, Conley admitted that he wrote the notes (*Atlanta Constitution*, 25 May 1913: 1). All told, Conley's story evolved over five separate affidavits until his final version emerged: he did write the notes, but Frank dictated them to him after killing Mary Phagan. At the trial, Conley reiterated this claim, explaining his willingness to help Frank "because he was a white man and my superintendent" (Dinnerstein 42). This version is the one around which the prosecution fashioned its reconstruction of the murder of Mary Phagan and which the jury would accept as being far enough beyond a reasonable doubt to convict Frank.

This central component of the prosecution's case against Frank raised more questions than it answered. Many observers of the trial, whether partisans or opponents of Frank, became fascinated with this matter and focused all their attention on the meanings of the murder notes. Did these notes accurately represent Black dialect? If so, could Frank possibly have dictated these notes so accurately? Or, on the other hand, did the notes contain racial clues that made it clear that mimetic imperfections in the dialect pointed suspicion back to a white author behind them? Was it plausible to consider that Frank had dictated "standard" English and the notes represented Conley's translation? What did "night witch" really refer to? If, as the prosecution claimed, the notes were the result of a collaborative effort, did they embody (or indeed add to or ameliorate) anxieties about criminal, or at least immoral, alliances of African American and Jew? In all, the notes provide a fascinating glimpse into popular attitudes about power and mediation as dramatized in the fields of literacy and literariness. Contesting interpretations of the notes were based not on positivistic data but rather in acts of faith; conclusions about the notes derived primarily from a priori racial (and regional) essentialisms that offer us insight into the general status of African Americans and Jews in the World War I era. The competing economies that structured the Frank case are nowhere more plainly observed than in the battle over the murder notes: differing conceptions of intelligence, power, and authenticity were ascribed to Leo Frank and Jim Conley in this contest and played a major role in constituting the public identities of the two men.

The notes received their most concentrated analysis during the appeals process, but some serious attention was paid to them at Frank's original trial. Prosecuting attorney Hugh Dorsey, following a line of argument that placed Frank as the mastermind of the crime, asked rhetorically whether "ever a negro lived on the face of the earth who, after having killed and robbed, or ravished and murdered a girl down in that dark basement, or down there in that area, would have taken up the time to have written these notes" (Dorsey 161). A few significant assumptions are being made here: first, a southern African American, unlike a northern Jew, would be aware of the inevitability of punishment for such a crime as this and would not play games with notes and such; he would hightail it out of town as quickly as possible, knowing that otherwise there would be no escape from the lynch mob. In this moment, Dorsey topples simple notions of ignorance and intelligence, for it is only the unlettered African American who can decipher competently the southern code of retribution.

But Frank and his supporters thought that the very existence of the notes pointed suspicion at Conley. In a letter written from prison, Frank reminded his correspondent that Conley at first denied his ability to write, which should create some suspicion, and moreover that it was unthinkable that a sensible white person would leave incriminating evidence at the scene of a crime.[2] C. P. Connolly argued similarly "the whole idea of the writing of the notes is so idiotic that no white man of intelligence, much less a Cornell graduate, would have conceived it" (88). Frank and his supporters never hesitated to activate just the sort of racist reasoning that would poison public opinion against him; nor did they always bother to recall just how tenuous was his status as white. Although, as we have seen, Frank never doubted that he would be taken to be a white man, much of the rhetoric in and around the case suggests that his whiteness was itself one of the questions being settled by the trial.

Partisans for the two men did not rely only on the acts of broad interpretation already mentioned. Dorsey also offered close readings of the texts, suggesting for instance that "Old Jim Conley, if he had written these notes, never would have said 'this negro did it by his self' . . . he would have said 'I done it.'" Dorsey then proceeded to quote numerous instances in the trial transcript when Conley used "done" instead of "did" (67). Dorsey is sharp: the use of "old" as an adjective paints Conley as a recognizable fantasy of the trusted, pliant African American of bygone days, while the picky (and, for the record, inaccurate) argument about "did" versus "done" establishes a triangle of southern insiders whose three points are Dorsey, Conley, and the jury.

One writer who petitioned for Frank's life called attention to the effectiveness of Conley's performance at the trial. To this observer Frank seemed a likelier suspect at first, primarily because Conley's "humble language like, 'Boss'" made him out "to be one of those old time negroes about seventy or seventy-five years old, who was raised by one of those Ante Bellum southern gentlemen, whose virtues [sic] truth and justice he acquired in youth and practiced in old age." The case took on a much different cast for this observer as the trial progressed and it was revealed that Conley was "a twenty-seven year old buck, and a person who was often for various misdeeds an inmate in jail."[3] Frank, then, looked less guilty if he was pitted directly against the "real" Jim Conley.

Confederate veteran Berry Benson wrote similarly of how Dorsey called Conley "'Old Jim' as though this base young negro was one of the old-time gray-headed darkeys whose vigilant faithfulness is woven into Confederate history, watchmen in the night who loved their masters and mistresses as they loved their God." This was repellent to Benson, given that "Conley is one of these salacious young negroes whose lustful eyes follow white women as they pass, deterred from attacking them only by fear of the noose and . . . revolver."[4] These contentions summarize neatly the developing connections being drawn between Conley's youth and the racial and sexual threat he posed, connections that would come into starker relief when Conley's language competence was demonstrated. Since Conley's testimony was so important to the prosecution's case it became necessary for Dorsey to convince the jury not only that Frank was a threatening newcomer to southern society but also that Conley was a familiar type. Drawing on the conventions of the minstrel show and the plantation-school novel, Dorsey insisted that Conley be understood within the category of "old negro." In turn, it fell to Frank's supporters to contend that Conley was a new kind of African American—anarchic, degraded, and dangerous: to them Conley was just the sort of "new Negro" who loafed, got drunk, and attacked white women.

A remarkable range of observers believed that many of the major questions raised by the Frank case—particularly those that articulated the competition of African American and Jew—could be profitably addressed through intense scrutiny of the original murder notes. Personal and professional interest in the notes made for strange bedfellows. One of the most notable enthusiasts of a theory that held that the very language of the notes removed suspicion from Conley as author (rather than simply Frank's stenographer) was James Weldon Johnson, the African American intellectual who, at the time, was a regular columnist for the *New York Age*. Writing in March of 1915, Johnson first established Conley's low intelligence; he then went on to argue that "if Conley is stupid and ignorant he belongs to a class of colored people that never, either in speaking or writing, uses the word 'Negro'" (*New York Age*, 11 Mar. 1915: 4). Unwittingly, Johnson joined Dorsey in depicting Conley's damaged literacy as his savior. The issue of "negro" versus "nigger" had been evaluated earlier by one of Frank's attorneys, Luther Rosser, who concluded that while "nigger" was the word commonly used by whites in Georgia, "'negro' is the first word the negro learns to spell at school, and that is the one word that he always pronounces correctly" (qtd. in *New York Times*, 4 Mar. 1914: 2).

The level of Conley's literacy was given deep attention at the trial, as Frank's attorneys attempted to demonstrate that Conley was more literate than he pretended. After being confronted with evidence that he had been observed reading newspapers, Conley admitted that there were "some little letters like 'dis' and 'dat' that I can read. The other things I don't understand" (*Brief of Evidence* at 59). During this cross-examination Conley insisted that even if he could read these words, he could not spell them himself. Here the minstrel caricaturing of Jim Conley seems most obvious. Eric Lott explains that a familiar scene in minstrel show "playlets" had Sambo Johnson being scorned by his fellow bootblacks after winning the lottery: these bootblacks ridiculed Johnson for putting on airs, commonly pointing out that he was reading his newspaper upside down (133).

The "dis" and "dat" issue was taken up by a number of other commentators as well. One of the more remarkable instances of Frank's two-year ordeal came in 1914 when Conley's lawyer announced that he now considered his client guilty, based on the evidence of the murder notes. William Smith privately printed an extensive analysis of the notes whose intent was to fix Conley as author. Among Smith's many unsupported contentions is that "Conley never uses dis and dat, and always uses this and that correctly and knows how to spell them and write them correctly."[5] Smith's fundamental tactic here is to strip Conley of the defense of dialect, and thereby strip him of the protection he had been offered on the pretext of being "Old Jim Conley," the trusted "darkey" of times gone by. Another Frank partisan took up the "dis" and "dat" (and "done" versus "did") question and employed particularly tortured reasoning: according to Berry Benson, although the average "Northern man is quite incapable of writing negro, he does know this, that 'dis and dat,' and 'done' (for did) are essentially negro. . . . Therefore, that the word used is 'did' . . . is evidence that Frank did not dictate the notes."[6] In other words, Frank was smart enough (even for a northern man) to do better dialect than that found in the murder notes. The logical end of this argument—that Conley wrote these poor imitations of dialect—is consistent with a rhetoric becoming familiar at this time that held that African Americans were not developing their "raw" materials into the "high" forms that might be built upon them.

Other linguistic aspects of the murder notes proved revealing when viewed through the correct lens. One anonymous pamphleteer suggested that the use of a double adjective style ("long tall," for instance) "was characteristic of Conley."[7] Two decades later this amateur anthropologist would have found impressive support in Zora Neale Hurston's "Characteristics of Negro Expression," in which Hurston suggested that the use of the "double descriptive" was one of the African American's three greatest contributions to American English.[8] William Smith also pointed out a number of less salutary characteristics, including Conley's lack of punctuation, use of monosyllables, repetition, incorrect spelling, and absence of capitalization.[9]

The prosecution came back to the issue of Conley's literacy during their redirect questioning. To prove he was indeed illiterate, Conley was asked to spell some words that included "George Washington," "Uncle Remus," and "Luxury." In response, Conley spelled "Uncle Remus" as "O-n-e R-i-n-e-s," "Luxury" as "L-u-s-t-r-i-s" and "George Washington" as "J-o-e W-i-s-h-t-o-n" (*Brief of Evidence* at 74). At first glance this performance is unremarkable — perfectly consistent, in fact, with the suggestion made by the prosecution that Conley was literate enough to take fractured dictation but not intelligent enough to think up the whole scheme.

A closer look at this spelling exam reveals it to be the most extraordinary moment of the entire Frank trial. In order to save himself and doom Frank, Conley was being asked to take, and fail, a literacy test. The first irony discovered here is that Conley's mandatory failure reverses the synonymity between literacy and liberty which was a central construct for so many (male) authors of slave narratives (Stepto 3–31). In more recent days the literacy test was familiar in its aspect as a tool used by white southerners to disqualify African Americans from voting in the post-Reconstruction era: the literacy requirement had been proposed by Hoke Smith in Georgia as recently as 1906, and an understanding clause (which holds that the prospective voter must explain a passage read to him) was included as part of a suffrage law in the state in 1908. The literacy test became so ubiquitous in these years as to have become a stock setup in African American humor. But now it became compelling for Dorsey to apply the literacy test as a means to liberate Conley: Conley's struggles with "standard" English proved that he was innocent. Frank, by contrast, was rendered more suspicious by the eloquence he displayed in a long statement he made in his own defense. Here, as elsewhere, received images of the Jew as sophisticated to the point of decadence were in effect.

This extraordinary moment also emphasizes the strange yet decisive role played by literary images and conventions in Frank's trial. The words Conley is asked to spell — "George Washington," "Uncle Remus," and "luxury" among them — narrate and interpret the events of the case itself. Each term seems to have an obvious analogue within the affair. "George Washington" evokes an image of the southern white patriarchy that has recently been shaken, specifically by the sexual violence allegedly connected to Mary Phagan's murder, and more generally by the advent of industrialization in the South. Dorsey himself stands in for the fathers during the trial: his role is to avenge the murder and possible rape of a southern daughter, and he carries out his responsibilities ably. Dorsey's authority derives concretely from institutional sanction but also from his mastery of racial politics within the case; his careful presentation of Conley as both "old" but also as a child demonstrates Dorsey's aptitude. Conley, of course, has been coerced to take the role of Uncle Remus in order to tell stories about the plantation, here represented by the factory. These stories are then framed by a white man (Dorsey) for a white audience (the jury). All through the trial, as I have noted, Dorsey labored to convince his listeners that Conley was just the sort of "old negro" memorialized by Joel Chandler Harris. (It probably bears mentioning that Harris first published his Uncle Remus stories in the pages of the *Atlanta Constitution*.) The final word of this series ("luxury") makes obvious reference to Frank's status as capitalist as well as to his alleged sensuality. Overall, Conley's performance, carefully guided by Dorsey, posits an alternative temporal sphere where Frank barely exists. Conley and Dorsey, in this scheme, understand each other and have a seemingly organic relationship; these two enacted dialogues throughout the trial, dialogues that expressed the proper workings of race relations and served as an antidote to the troubling image of the chaos that obtained in the National Pencil Company factory. Frank, with no fixed racial status, with alien racial and class affect, is read out of southern culture through Conley's spelling exam.

As Conley explained the matter, "Uncle Remus," "George Washington," and "Luxury" (along with "Thomas Jefferson" and "Magnolia") were the names of pencils produced in the factory. Taken together it seems certain that the pencil manufacturers were quite consciously evoking plantation imagery to sell their products. More to the point, Conley claimed in his testimony that he had practiced copying out the names of these pencils at Frank's request. Without explaining exactly why Frank wanted him to learn to write, Conley's implication was clear: the Jewish factory manager could use the increased literacy of the African American janitor for his own benefit (*Brief of Evidence* at 74; Golden 136–37). The Mary Phagan drama took place in a *pencil* factory, we need to recall, and it should be noted that in addition to providing Conley with direct access to white women, Leo Frank also furnished the African American man with the tools of literacy. The connection between the literacy of the African American male and the threat he posed was made explicit by one white supremacist newspaper in Texas that argued, "statistics show that while many more negroes learn to read and write each year, more white women are outraged and murdered."[10]

The amount of attention paid to these seemingly arcane linguistic issues raised by the notes illuminates a fairly frantic attempt to freeze a hierarchy of racial characteristics that would ease the unnamed yet powerful fears of disorder that the crime and its accompanying details had raised. Reflections on what type of person would be most capable of knowing African American in-group cultural material and reproducing dialect became the center of this curious discourse. As I outline this discussion, I am most interested in drawing attention to what is missing from the conversation: for all of the bizarre arguments put forth, no one ever claimed that Frank was particularly well suited to imitate this African American form because he was a Jew. In an age of Irving Berlin's ascendance ("Alexander's Ragtime Band" was a hit of 1911) it was becoming common to assume that something about Jews (their similar marginality, their ancient strain of melancholy) fitted them well to interpret African American culture. Perhaps a certain chauvinism on the part of southern whites with respect to their own special understanding of things African American helped them resist this increasingly powerful cultural construct.

The most explicit presentation of the contention that Frank was far too distant from Conley in a cultural sense to have dictated these notes came in Berry Benson's self-published "Five Arguments in the Frank Case." His case deserves to be quoted at some length:

> As the son of an owner of slaves till my 18th year, then as a Confederate soldier more than four years, and since the war as a citizen of Augusta, Georgia; of Austin, Texas; of New York City; and of Washington City, employing negroes, I know somewhat of negro character and of negro manner of expression. And I know somewhat of the white man's ability (and inability) to imitate him. And it is my candid and fixed opinion, after careful scrutiny and patient study of these two notes, that there is not a white man, either North or South, who could have dictated them. They are negro throughout, beyond the white man's ability to imitate. If Edgar Allan Poe, a genius with his pen, a southern man, failed, as he did fail, in his story of "The Gold Bug," to write properly the dialect of the Carolina coast negro, how could a northern man, in the South but a few years, possibly express negro lingo? There is not one northern writer who attempts to write negro but makes a ridiculous failure. He cannot even read it; I have to stop my ears with my fingers when I hear him try.[11]

Much in this case points us to the conclusion that Jews and African Americans were conceived of as racially aberrant — that is, as different from an implicit norm. Still, these fairly generic similarities between Jews and African Americans should not blind us to the very real differences that marked imagery surrounding the groups. There is nothing in this passage just quoted to suggest that Jews and African Americans had a special line of communication to each other — far from it. In fact, the primary category for Frank when it comes to his knowledge of African American culture and language is "white" man, while the secondary category is "northern." But Edgar Allan Poe — there was a man who would have at least had a fighting chance to write a murder note in the voice of Jim Conley!

Benson gains authority here by subtly positioning himself as the most competent reader of this case. Most important is his positive claim that the notes are "negro throughout." We might be tempted to ask of course why an intelligent white man who can recognize "negro throughout" would not be able to imitate it, but Benson's underlying argument is clear enough: an academic recognition of "negro throughout" is very different from an ability to create the same without an appearance of artifice. In what may have been a response to Benson's claims about the dialect in the notes, a Georgia state senator wrote to Governor Slaton to argue that the notes, rather than being "in" dialect, represented a failure of mimetic art. The notes, according to A. H. Foster, could not have been written by any "white man familiar with negro phraseology and negro dialect. Just what you would expect from a white reared and educated in some other section than the South. As you are aware, no writer from any other section has ever succeeded in negro dialect."[12]

It is little surprise that commentators on the Frank case insisted upon a rigid separation of Black and white cultural expressions. Analysis of blackface minstrelsy in our century has often been hampered by the presumption that racialized expressions must have their roots exclusively in either Black culture or white culture. In fact, it is only recently that a scholar of stage blackface, W. T. Lhamon, has made the paradigm-shifting suggestion that early black-face styles—particularly in dance—were the fruits of interracial collaborations. The murder notes found by Mary Phagan were the kind of dialect pieces that had been a staple of stage blackface since the mid-nineteenth century, and later became regular features in newspapers and magazines. But familiar or not, the use of dialect in the Frank case offered observers raw material out of which they made strong arguments about the relationship of Jews, African Americans, and white Americans in the modern city.

The real center of the controversy came with attempts to explain the presence of the phrase "night witch" in the murder notes. According to Leonard Dinnerstein very little attention was paid to the locution "play like the night witch did it" at Frank's original trial, because most people "automatically assumed that the expression referred to the night watchman." The conjecture was that Frank was attempting to direct suspicion toward Newt Lee, the recently hired night watchman at the factory. But in an extraordinary motion for a new trial filed before the Georgia Supreme Court, Frank's lawyers offered a simpler explanation: "Night witch" meant "night witch." Ignoring Conley's spelling performance at the original trial, one of Frank's attorneys concluded that "although the author of the murder notes had made many spelling errors, he had not made any in pronunciation"; even more telling, this lawyer discovered an African American superstition that held that when children "cry out in their sleep at night, it means that the night witches are riding them, and if you don't go and wake them up, they will be found next morning strangled to death, with a cord around their necks" (Dinnerstein 87, 90). Just like Mary Phagan!

As many people saw things, Leo Frank ("a Cornell graduate and a Northern man, unused all his life to association with negroes until his advent in Atlanta, and then only in the remotest business association" [Connolly 88]) could not possibly know anything of this superstition. One of Frank's lawyers underlined just this point in an appeal before Judge Leonard Roan for a new trial, suggesting that Frank had "very little knowledge of negroes" and was in reality "almost a stranger here." There was no chance, then, that Frank could have manipulated the "dark vernacular of the negro" for his own use (Arnold 51–52).

Two significant presumptions mark this line of thinking. The first is that Frank had little contact with actual African American people—a patently false claim given his contacts in the factory and in his home, where an African American woman served as cook. In fact, one major controversy in the early investigation broke out when this woman, Minola McKnight, was brought in for questioning by the police. McKnight gave an affidavit (perhaps under extreme duress) that supported the case against Frank. No matter how the affidavit was secured, the obvious point to make is that everyone concerned accepted the basic premise that McKnight and Frank shared the same social space.[13]

The second assumption is that folklore, stage and literary traditions, speech habits—in a word, the culture of African Americans—would be invisible and inaccessible to a "white" American such as Frank, this notwithstanding the fact that the lawyer who made the discovery about "night witch" was himself a Jew (Cahan 501). A cursory glance at the *Atlanta Constitution* shows how absurd the insistence on segregated culture was. On the Sunday morning that Mary Phagan's body was found in the National Pencil Company factory basement, the *Constitution* printed "humorous" sermons supposedly delivered by one Br'er Williams: "Money can't open de last gate for you but it kind

give you a high old time ridin' till you git to de gate" (26 Apr. 1913: 6F).
Even in the face of such evidence, Frank's people tried to establish Frank's
"whiteness" (and I mean that doubly here to signify his racial standing and
his innocence) by demonstrating his distance from even the most trivial constituent of American culture that might be traceable to African Americans.
But one story told by the Frank case was that, Jim Crow laws and Jim Crow
practices notwithstanding, Black and white southerners were mixing in the
New South factory.

James Weldon Johnson was observing the public conversation about the
murder notes and did not hesitate to join it. Johnson thought it absurd to re-
solve life-and-death matters based on the presence of dialect in the murder
notes. In a *New York Age* column, Johnson quoted an editorial from another
paper that contended that "Frank might have had cunning enough to allow
Conley to spell as he pleased, but as a Northerner it is scarcely conceivable
that he would have thought of introducing the reference to the Negro superstition concerning the night witch." In the 1920s and 1930s Johnson frequently would look to the years just preceding World War I as a time when
white (and particularly Jewish) appropriation of African American cultural
forms became epidemic. So, in response to the oft-repeated claim that Frank
could not have known anything of African American culture, Johnson instead
suggested that "it would be the most natural thing for a northerner living in
the South, as did Frank, to become familiar with the various Negro superstitions. In fact, these superstitions have been given such wide circulation
through the 'Uncle Remus' stories and other mediums that there are northerners who never lived in the South who can glibly write in poetry and prose
about 'night witches' and 'hants' and 'conjure people'" (*New York Age*, 11
Mar. 15: 4).

First Conley took on the role of Uncle Remus to strengthen the state's
case against Frank and ease the pressure on himself; now Johnson enlists the
very existence of the Uncle Remus stories to argue that Frank was close enough
to African American cultural forms to imitate them. Johnson harvests some
specific and some general protest material here. His most obvious point seems
to be that if outsiders would plunder African American culture for material
gain and fame (as Joel Chandler Harris did—and in Atlanta at that), Frank

certainly would not hesitate to do the same if it meant saving his own life. But if we read Johnson's analogy in reverse order—from Frank's alleged use of dialect back to Uncle Remus—it is possible to read in it the contention that "murder" is one way of conceptualizing the appropriation of African American cultural materials.[14]

Johnson's argument underscores two related questions being negotiated around the actual texts of the Mary Phagan murder notes. First, was there some recognizable mode of speaking or writing (and hence, it would seem, being) that could be classified only as "Negro"? And second, who had access to this partly hidden language? Johnson's stance, not surprisingly, was predicated on the assumption that one could no longer speak of a discrete or hidden African American culture, existing somewhere outside the mainstream of a broader "American" culture.

One respondent to Johnson's editorial in the *Age* took the argument even further, adopting a strategy whereby Conley would be saved, though the race be damned. The argument made here was that it was not only possible that a non-African American had devised these clever murder notes, it was necessarily so. Conley could not have been responsible for this creative act, for the race as a whole had produced "about only three descriptive writers of note." Once again, a version of literary history (or lack thereof) is being summoned in an attempt to settle life-and-death questions. This letter to the *Age* goes on to clarify its message by suggesting "the race has not been fully stimulated by those economic *impulses* which develop the mind in detail, modes of thought and expression" (*New York Age*, 25 Mar. 1915: 4; emphasis in original). This interesting argument leaves us only to utter the unasked question: which race has been fully stimulated by those economic impulses that develop the mind?

James Weldon Johnson's insights might be expanded here to take note of the fact that white people have frequently mined African American folk culture for more than simple monetary gain. Indeed, as Gladys-Marie Fry explains, the appropriation of African American folk beliefs was a common modality of social control both during and after slavery (52–58). (One need only look to the authenticating strategies of blackface minstrelsy—which featured white actors who presented horrible racist caricatures on stage and then claimed they were essentially offering documentary—to discover how the use of allegedly "real" Black materials could serve to reinforce oppressive racial practices.) According to Fry, slave masters and their various deputies, as well as various postbellum whites, deployed an intimate knowledge of African American culture in order to regulate the movement of African Americans. Armed with the knowledge that African Americans feared night riders, white southerners perpetuated these occult narratives by patrolling slaves while disguised as ghosts; the apparel of the Ku Klux Klan is an obvious manifestation of this system of policing. If such opportunistic impersonations materially worked to confine African Americans, the content of the night witch tales also offered a cautionary message that individualized and sexualized the diffuse patterns of racial domination in the South. The action of being ridden, sometimes after being turned on all fours, reminded African Americans that white "witches" might demonstrate their power by violating the bodies of African American women (Fry 52–58; Hughes and Bontemps 199–200).

But we must be careful here not to flatten out the development of this social drama. White people did not simply overhear the tale of the witch and incorporate it into an existing supervisory scheme. To begin, it is not altogether clear where the tales of witch riding came from, and Richard Dorson, for one, argues that these stories actually have a European origin (236–44; see also Fishkin 81–83). As with many questions of origins, the real issue here is usage: if witch tales served as an educational tool for African Americans, so did they continue to perform the work of surveillance for white people interested in controlling African Americans.

The back-and-forth construction of this field of interracial activity is perhaps best observed in the famous scene of Jim's "witching" in *Huckleberry Finn*. In this early moment of the novel Tom Sawyer decides to abuse the napping Jim; he does this by hanging Jim's hat on a branch above him. In essence Tom has no goal outside of exerting the privileges of his white boyhood, but Jim seems to gain most from the sham witching: "Afterwards Jim said the witches bewitched him and put him in a trance, and rode him all over the State, and then set him under the trees again and hung his hat on a limb to show who done it. And next time Jim told it he said they rode him down to New Orleans; and after that, everytime he told it he spread it more and more, till by-and-by he said they rode him all over the world and tired him most to death, and his back was all over saddle-boils." From this petty act of social control by the white boy, Jim extracts a fable of chosenness and mobility that enhances his status in the community: "Niggers would come miles to hear Jim tell about it, and he was more looked up to than any nigger in that country" (Twain 16). The insertion of a witch riding in *Huckleberry Finn* discloses that white people—including perhaps a "Cornell graduate" if he took the right classes—could know about such tales; it also emphasizes that contests of power take place within these folkloric narratives *and* around their dissemination. In this light the assertion by Frank's lawyer that his client could not possibly have known about the night witch should be taken not as a positivistic observation but rather as a measured disavowal of Frank's access to the complex network of southern racial interactions. During the trial Frank suffered because his foreignness was coded negatively as excess: too much money, too much liberty, too much intelligence. In the appeal, attorney Henry Alexander attempted to refashion Frank's "difference" as lack, an ignorance that might clear the northern Jew of any criminal activities that expressed, however incidentally, southern folkways.

Of course a reference to "night witch" might not *really* exist in the Mary Phagan murder notes: Conley, who spelled "George Washington" as "Joe Wishton," might—as many of his contemporaries thought—simply have been trying to pin blame on Newt Lee, the night watchman. But once stitched backed into the record of the trial by Frank's lawyer, "night witch" came to seem a perfectly apt predictor of the competition of available villains that characterized the Frank case. As a historical site, the lore of the night witch was itself a locus of conflict between whites and African Americans. In the appeal crafted by Frank's lawyers, "night witch" continued to accommodate interracial struggles for control.

The variety of codes that might be at work in the notes is truly staggering, even granting the one seemingly indisputable point that they are in Conley's handwriting. Whatever the historical consensus now tells us about Frank's innocence, it is important to remember that during his lifetime there was a widespread belief (or at least a will to believe) in his guilt. With this in mind, what might the murder notes generally, and the "night witch" reference specifically, communicate about the relative status of Frank and Conley? Following the narrative offered at Frank's trial (that Frank dictated the notes to Conley to cover his own guilt) presents the most interesting scenario. What does it mean, finally, that Frank's conviction relied in part on an argument that held that he said *something* that Conley wrote down as "night witch"? The most fascinating possibility to consider is that it was Frank who said "night watchman" in a crude attempt to implicate Newt Lee, and Conley who *purposely* rendered it as "night witch" in a final bid to subvert the man who held so much power over him. (And I don't mean here to try to imagine what actually happened, but merely to suggest a connotative chain that might have been activated by the murder notes and by Henry Alexander's appeal on the evidence of them.) As Conley put it, he followed Frank's direction because Frank was his boss and a white man; the message of "night witch," then, can be taken as a desperate effort on Conley's part to tell his imagined readers that he was being "patrolled" by Leo Frank. Similarly interesting is the possibility that Conley invented all of it by himself in a *conscious* attempt to confuse the white authorities; this is the schema developed by Barbara Lebow and Frank Wittow in their 1967 play inspired by the case (see especially 80–81).

Henry Alexander's revival of the specter of the "night witch" might have reminded the court, then, that older plantation dramas were now played out in the factory, and that in this case a northern Jew had displaced the southern white to take over the starring role as master. Alexander might have been correct in his argument that the "night witch" reference was inaccessible to Leo Frank (and even this is unlikely), but he failed to see that fixing Frank as an outsider led Frank down a dangerous trail: Alexander helped construct a vision of the South that had room *only* for Black and white. By marginalizing the Jewish man's role as a significant third term in the racial calculus, Alexander promoted the reunion of Black and white southerners that was made possible (and perhaps necessary) by the murder of a young white woman in a factory owned and operated by Jews.

In 1914 another series of documents somewhat mysteriously came to light that offered further evidence as to the literacy of Jim Conley; a number of letters written by Conley to a woman he met while in jail, Annie Maud Carter, were "discovered" by a detective who had been hired by the Frank defense effort. William J. Burns, a well-known private eye, would never tell how he came into possession of this set of letters, and Conley denied writing them, but there is strong evidence that he was indeed the author (Dinnerstein 102–3).[15]

No matter what the origin of the letters, they offered contemporary observers another opportunity to consider the character of Conley (and by comparison, Leo Frank), and they allow us further insight into the uses of racial comparison in determining guilt for Mary Phagan's murder. The Conley letters provide access to the central issue of status I have been slowly circling around: how was the Frank case manipulated (by African Americans, Jews, and other Americans) to carve out race-specific identities for Jews and African Americans, and most particularly, how did each identity rely on the existence of a useful correlate in the other group? With the appearance of this next set of notes, it becomes more clear that even if the Frank case may ultimately have led to some *organized* alliance-making between African Americans and Jews, the affair itself was marked most by an overt competition between the two groups. It is in this aspect that I read the Frank case as expressing a prime modality of Black-Jewish interactions — one that is erratic, unpredictable, and situational.

The letters attributed to Conley were considered too vulgar to print in Atlanta newspapers of the time. If Conley did not write the letters, and they represented a ploy on the part of Frank's supporters, then they miscalculated; the lack of news coverage allowed the letters to disappear from public consciousness almost as soon as they appeared. This cycle of letters consisted primarily of attempts by Conley to seduce Annie Maud Carter. In his first letter, Conley wrote: "Baby, you ought not never said anything to me about your hipped, [?] why my dick went clean across my cell, and I read it all night, your letter. I could not sleep. . . . every time read that my long dick got on a hard, . . . I love you so much and if I could put my sweet long dick in your hipped, I think I could make Mama call me Papa, one time." The second letter must have seemed to Frank's advocates even more damning of Conley: "I want you to keep your ass right there because it is good and you told me this last night in your letter, that two hours fucking on your big fat ass would stop all of this argument. . . . if you let papa put his long ugly dick up in your fat ass and play on your right and left hip, just like a monkey playing on a trapeze, then Honey Papa will be done played hell with you. . . . I want to stick my long dick in your ass. . . . Give your heart to God and your ass to me."[16]

On the linguistic level, we find that Conley does indeed favor the double-adjective style William Smith noticed in the murder notes; further, there are other places in the letters, contrary to Hugh Dorsey and James Weldon Johnson, where Conley employs the word "Negro" as opposed to "Nigger" (Dinnerstein 102). But what is most striking about these letters is that they reactivate the issue of perversion (especially with Conley's use of the verb "play") that had such a central role in Frank's original conviction and formed the partial basis for one of his appeals.[17] As was usual in this case, when Frank's supporters went on the offensive they merely co-opted the racist rhetoric that had helped doom their man and applied it to Jim Conley. Berry Benson, for instance, concluded that Conley's letters to Annie Maud Carter proved that he was a "beastly sodomite."[18] This was the missing piece in the defense claim that Conley, and not Frank, was responsible for the crime: where Conley had provided the clue to Frank's motivation (his addiction to oral sex), now Conley revealed that perhaps it was he who did not perform as "other men" did, preferring his intercourse to be anal. Since the newspapers and the testimony at the trial were never all that clear on what it meant to be a pervert (or a sodomite) Conley's fixation on Annie Maud Carter's "fat ass" might fit the bill just as well as Frank's purported obsessions had. But since Conley's letters never entered the public consciousness, the comfortable thought that he was illiterate continued to go unchallenged.

Much of the rhetoric surrounding the Leo Frank affair had to do with questions of relative power, a point Nancy MacLean makes brilliantly clear in her study of how the case exacerbated an ongoing battle for the control of southern women. One key contested power relationship that permeated the case, although rarely breaking through the coded language in any manifest way, was that which pitted African American "ignorance" versus Jewish "intellect." The pivotal concern (what type of person would do this to a poor, defenseless Gentile/white girl?) was distilled, as I have been outlining, into small doses of concentrated elements. The circumstance of the murder notes, with the attendant debates about the relative literacy, creativity, and mimetic abilities of African Americans and Jews, articulated embedded misgivings about the agency of these two groups. Much attention has been paid to a linear theory of African American and Jewish relations, a theory rooted in examples of liberal Jews encouraging the general progress and protection of African Americans as a way of insuring their own position.[19] But little has been made over more complicated examples of the relatedness of the status of the two groups. In the tangled web surrounding the Frank case one dominant thread of comparison worked to create an impression of safety about African Americans rooted mainly in their familiarity to southern whites (as when Dorsey referred to Conley as "old Jim"), while by implication depicting Jews as dangerous, based on their alien ways. In the instance of the murder notes, more specifically, Jim Conley's innocence was proved by his ignorance. Illiteracy, real or imagined, marked Conley as within the pale, and served as an amulet to ward off the suspicion of guilt.

Predictably, just as Conley's illiteracy certified his guiltlessness, so too was Frank's culpability revealed by his intellect. An early Atlanta newspaper report described Frank, with apparent disdain, as "a fluent talker" (qtd. in Dinnerstein 6), and a sympathetic *New York Times* account suggested that even Frank's supporters would characterize him as "shrewd" and "egotistical" (*New York Times*, 23 Feb. 1915: 9). That Frank could prepare a precise accounting report, or write a dispassionate letter to his uncle up North after killing Mary Phagan, confirmed that he had superior faculties, and must also have authored these bizarre notes. William Smith, whom I mentioned above as Conley's traitorous lawyer, recognized how large the claims for Frank's skills had become: "It is a pity" he wrote, "that the people cry out for the 'JEW'S' blood, because, it is a pity to kill such a LANGUAGE GENIUS, that he can look into negro Conley's face and grasp in two minutes and a half, [Conley's] LANGUAGE ."[20] As Smith's evocative image has it, the Jew and the African American are left frozen into untenable positions, each gazing into the other's face in an attempt only to find an alibi. Once the territory has been established, there is not even a rhetorical escape route.

The ultimate import of this case — as with so many installments in African American-Jewish relatedness — is that it encouraged so many Jews, African

Americans, and others to conceive of the two groups as mutually defining. The Leo Frank case did not bring African Americans and Jews to fullest visibility as equal partners in a conscious alliance. Instead, each was made to appear as a distorted negative image of the other, the African American and the Jew existing primarily as sordid companions in a debased association.

"A ROMAN HOLIDAY"

Making Leo Frank Signify

In Atlanta a holiday, an exorcism complete with iced tea and shortcake.
Michelle Cliff, Free Enterprise

After listening to this confusion of voices and trying to untangle all the inconsistencies and contradictions in interpretations of the Frank affair, we discover at the end that it was about confusion, inconsistency, and contradiction. The year of Frank's lynching, 1915, came in back of three decades of mass immigration to the United States and the influx of industrial capitalism into the South, not to mention a passel of other epoch-making innovations in the American scene.

What has not been sufficiently appreciated is how charged the entire atmosphere around the affair had been made by the fact that it upset the precise racial and ethnic hierarchies by which so many Americans had previously set store. If there was anti-Semitism in the affair, so too was their anti-Black racism — as well as a class-based antagonism against "Mary's people" (which some would claim is also an ethnic bias of sorts). In studying the Frank case I am impressed most by how often the deepest complexities resolved into rather straightforward and practical (rather than ethical) issues: Who would it make sense to hate more at this moment, an African American or a Jew? Or, on a different tack, if African Americans and Jews were going to be hated by the same people — albeit at different times and for different reasons — was it worthwhile for the two groups to combine forces?

One image suggests the difficulties we face in searching for any simple conclusion about the racial and ethnic competition that saturated this case. When the guilty verdict was announced at the end of Frank's trial there was great rejoicing all over Atlanta; C. P. Connolly described it as "a Roman holiday." One of the largest crowds gathered in front of the National Pencil Company factory and "cake-walked" for an hour (Connolly 19). To celebrate the conviction of a northern Jew for the murder of a young white woman, primarily on the testimony of a southern African American man who was also suspected of the crime, these white southerners did a dance invented by African American slaves to mock the pretensions of their white masters.

Leo Frank never climbed the gallows from which he was meant to hang, but the structure did not go to waste: in July of 1915 an African American man convicted of an unrelated crime was hanged on Frank's gallows (Cahan 559). This incidental detail reminds us that the Frank case gave rise to associations of African Americans and Jews that ultimately eclipsed all of the frantic distancing strategies intended to mark off the boundaries between the two groups. As Frank's tribulations wore on, it became evident that the affair coupled African Americans and Jews in a number of significant ways. These linkages were made concretely (for instance, in the fight for expansion of due-process protections) but even more pervasively as a rhetorical tendency. The Leo Frank case, especially after Frank's lynching, provided a frame in which a variety of social and political issues could be put on display.

In this final section, then, I want to explore how "Leo Frank" — inside and outside of quotation marks — was made to signify both during his appeals process and after his death. As long as Frank lived it remained difficult for African Americans and Jews to make common cause, because to free Frank was to doom Conley. Because of the competition over the actual bodies of the two men, each group tended to describe the other as belonging to an absolutely distinct social sphere — Frank was an overprivileged capitalist and Conley was a vicious Black criminal. But with the disappearance of Frank from the physical scene — that is, with his lynching — a new vocabulary was worked out that enabled his plight, his very specifically Jewish story, to be converted into a Black story. After a brief look at the disparate attempts made to separate Jim Conley and Leo Frank, I will conclude with a consideration of Frank's lynching as an inspiration for Black-Jewish unification.

There are ways in which the partisan reactions to the Frank case seem a figment of an addled conspiracy theorist's dream: with white southerners acting as a manipulative "third force," African Americans and Jews undertook a skirmish whose most significant effect would be to make each group seem more foreign and marginalized and less ready than before to take their place as citizens. While the most optimistic visions of Black-Jewish relations often imply that the alliance serves progressive functions only, in the Leo Frank case the arduous negotiations surrounding the clash of these two groups functioned mostly to divert attention away from more pressing questions about how power was being distributed in the New South.

As mentioned earlier, and as Eugene Levy seconds, this matter encouraged Jews and African Americans, two "outsider" groups, to endorse available negative images about each other in a search for minority-group primacy. Without attempting to answer the chicken-and-egg question ("Who started the name-calling?"), I think it is clear, as Nancy MacLean has written, that what "proved most decisive in shaping blacks' attitudes was the strategy of Frank's defense: a virulent racist offense against . . . Jim Conley" (924). Frank's lawyers employed racial epithets at every turn, and, as I have discussed, capitalized on much the same sort of racist thinking that helped to turn public opinion against their man. With the assistance of hindsight and numerous fictionalized versions of the case (Ward Greene's *Death in the Deep South* and the movie made from it, Oscar Micheaux's *Murder in Harlem*, and Richard Kluger's *Members of the Tribe*), it is surprising that Frank's lawyers did not instead propose a "third-man" theory. If they had fastened suspicion on a poor white, such as John M. Gantt (a former employee of the factory) or Arthur Mullinax (a streetcar conductor) — both early suspects (*Atlanta Constitution*, 28 and 29 Apr. 1913: 1) — they might have avoided not only the perils attending the competition of organized interest groups but also the staging of a racial drama in which Conley was relatively safe. Kluger's answer — that the crime was committed by a powerful southern white man (an extrapolation based on the real-life Herbert Schiff, the assistant superintendent of the factory) — seems less satisfying, given the way the trial was made to act as an opportunity for southern white men to regain lost power. For all the talk of Conley as a "friendless Negro" it seems clear that he was protected by his ability to play a role that was familiar to white southerners. Performing as an "old Negro," Conley offered the reassurance that aliens generated all evil existing in the New South.[1]

What needs to be stressed here is how completely stereotyped Conley was; for Frank, his attorneys, and most spectators, even African Americans, Conley had no individual identity. On the other hand, while Frank was often referred to as "the Jew," and the particularities of his appearance and character often became muddled or conflated with handy stereotypes, his individuality was never in question. Conley, on the other hand, was almost always treated as if he was one of the two most familiar minstrel show types: the credulous and wholly unreliable (rural) Jim Crow — the one Solicitor-General Dorsey conjured up when he said that "the oftener the negro changed his story, the more reliable it was likely to be" — or the pretentious, malaprop-ridden (urban) joker, Zip Coon/Jim Dandy, represented best by Conley's testimony as to which words he could spell (Connolly 51). In this respect the question of whether Conley was coached in his testimony or not becomes moot; his effectiveness at the trial was based on his already knowing what was expected of him. And what was expected of Conley above all was that he shift loyalties from one boss, Leo Frank, to a more appropriate one, Hugh Dorsey.

Implicit in comparisons of Frank and Conley was a notion that they inhabited different worlds. Where Frank was considered by most observers as a modern man (perhaps too modern), guided by logic and recognizable motive, Conley was depicted as prerational, naive, possessed of a certain native intelligence but no more — in short, as a member of the "folk." This interpretive framework is seen nowhere more clearly than in the parcel of suggestions made by Frank's supporters, aimed at tricking Conley into confessing that he was responsible for the murder of Mary Phagan.

These correspondents were convinced that eliciting a full confession from Conley was only a matter of applying a little folk wisdom. One anonymous writer reminded Lucille Frank, Leo's wife, that "Negroes are prone to confess to their misdeeds when they are [desperately] sick or dying." Simply arrange "to have something given him to make him sick a little and then tell him he was...about to die" and he would confess.[2] The assumption in such letters was, for one reason or another, that Conley's guilt had already been established for careful observers, and now only needed to be actively demonstrated. Mrs. F. G. Fleur wrote to Lucille Frank that, "of course the nigger Jim Conley is the guilty one, or he *never* would have written those notes. If someone could dope his food or a drink and make him *very* sick at his stomach, he would vomit, and have his [doctor], in the scheme of course, so he could tell him 'he surely is going to die, he cannot recover,' and he had better tell all he knows, so as to have his conscience clear when he dies. I do believe that nigger would confess if he thought he was going to die."[3] Even one letter writer who identified himself as "a Boy 16 years old" found it plain that "this negro committed this crime" and suggested employing a physician to poison Conley in order to extract a confession.[4] There is a level of confidence about these letters — a sense of utter certainty embedded in the very fact of them — that transcends their specific content. After all, these well-meaning correspondents were writing to a woman whose husband was suffering under sentence of death. Built into such letters is a reminder of the essential difference between Black and white: the importance of Jewishness as a subset of white or distinct category is sidestepped and any chance that Frank and Conley might be seen as similarly persecuted is foreclosed.

This unarticulated worldview comes through even more clearly in two letters, one to Lucille Frank, and one to Luther Z. Rosser (one of Frank's lawyers) that fantasize resolutions of this case as if it were a Gothic fiction. Both letters were written during the period when the Georgia State Prison Commission and Governor Slaton were deciding whether to grant the commutation that represented Frank's last hope. The letter to Lucille Frank reads, in part, as follows: "The negroes are all superstitious, and advantage might be taken of that fact to obtain a confession from the negro, Conley. If some clever detective could watch his chance, and appear to Conley in the guise of the ghost of Mary Phagan, threatening vengeance worse than death if he did not confess to the crime, he would no doubt get incriminating evidence, if not a complete confession."[5] In responding to a case in which so many taboos were broken, the idea of cross-dressing obviously did not seem like a very big transgression. I. P. W. Glenn wrote attorney Rosser a letter worthy of the early nineteenth-century American gothic novelist, Charles Brockden Brown, suggesting that if Frank's friends "want vindication" they should employ a good ventriloquist. The ventriloquist should be directed to haunt Jim Conley, "imitating Mary Fagan [sic] cry-groans and then the Devils [sic] laugh" until Conley finally tells the truth.[6]

Of course there was never any suggestion that a similar test be made of Frank; the assumption behind all of these claims is that they are applicable only to the superstitious African American man and not to the hyperrational pencil factory manager who used a large portion of his speaking time in court to describe the intricacies of preparing a balance sheet (*Brief of Evidence* at 174). In sum, this approach to the case positioned African Americans outside of civil society, living in an older world where the logical give-and-take of cross-examination could not possibly have any relevance. That most of these letters were addressed to Lucille Frank seems significant as well; her correspondents no doubt found it more likely that the plots they suggested would have resonance with the faithful, long-suffering wife than with her accountant-husband.[7] Newspapers unsympathetic to Frank frequently referred to his supporters as "sentimental," and it seems that many of those writing letters that backed Frank were indeed deriving some strategic ideas from female-identified literary materials.

At the same time as these letters were being written — letters that pitted the Jew as modern man versus the African American as historical anachronism — some African American journalists and intellectuals were using the controversy surrounding the release of D. W. Griffith's *Birth of a Nation* as a way of entering and redefining the public debate over the fates of Leo Frank and Jim Conley (Williamson 472). The dispute over whether *Birth of a Nation* ought to be released regardless of its inflammatory racist content presented observers with a handy interpretive analogy for the Frank case. To draw parallels between the prejudice that infused Griffith's film and the prejudice accompanying the Frank affair (whether anti-Semitism at his trial or later racist attempts to pin blame on Conley) was most of all a rhetorical gambit that deflected attention away from the principals and details of the case.

Along with the automobile, motion pictures were perhaps the most potent symbol of modernization in America.[8] To insist that this particular film had relevance to the Leo Frank case transformed the conversation from the either/or competition I have sketched out (either modern Jew or antiquated African American) to a both/and model. In employing this analogy, African American leaders recognized and tacitly resisted the subject/object conception that obtained in most considerations of the Frank/Conley contest, and demanded an equal place in the wild world of modernity.

The connection made between the film and the murder case derived from the involvement of Jews, most notably Louis B. Mayer, in the distribution of *Birth of a Nation*. African American newspapers saw support for and profit from a perniciously racist film as a repudiation of the universal humanism with which Frank's defenders sometimes attempted to cloak themselves (Gabler 90–91). In short, if it was wrong for southern whites to persecute Frank for his foreignness, so was it wrong to contribute to the persecution of African Americans sure to result from the powerful propaganda in this film. According to Hasia Diner some leading Jews did protest the release of *Birth of a Nation*: Joel Spingarn, Lillian Wald, and Jacob Schiff all "worked actively on an NAACP committee which implored the National Board of Censorship in Moving Pictures to withhold sanction of the film" (134). One Jewish magazine opposed these efforts, arguing that the film was actually "a compliment to the black man of today" because it demonstrated how far he had come since the days just after slavery (qtd. in Diner 103). These contretemps notwithstanding, African American newspapers saw mostly that some Jews were reaping financial gain from this movie, and generalized from there that Jews per se were not interested in broad-based social justice. Others were less interested in the financial backers of the movie and more concerned with its substantive message.

Though some tentative connections were established earlier in 1915, it was the lynching of Frank that underscored the relationship between the movie and racial violence in the actual world.[9] A group of African American civil rights leaders represented by William Monroe Trotter issued a press release that stated in part that "the Frank lynching should put an end to the 'Birth of a Nation' photo-play where the 'Gus' scene is the exact photo-type of the

Frank lynching with approval." This declaration concluded positively, "No one can consistently approve of the 'Birth of a Nation' and condemn the lynching of Frank."[10] Unlike the African American editorialists who directed their attention to Jewish financial support for the movie, these leaders were disquieted above all by what they saw as an obvious correlation between received film images and tangible behavior. This press release cleverly elides the difference in racial status of the movie's lynching victim and Leo Frank: violence begets violence, they argue, and once lynching fever takes hold, finer distinctions (African American versus Jew, for instance) might not have much meaning. This form of logic would be developed by numerous observers who saw in Frank's murder proof that lynching had so infected southerners' minds that they could no longer respect racial differences. In a different sense, it also demonstrates a common move to incorporate Leo Frank's lynching into a distinct African American historical narrative of racial persecution. After a death by lynching, the Jew's body could just as well be Black.

The fullest condemnation of the Jewish financial interest in Griffith's movie came with a long editorial in the *Indianapolis Freeman* of August 28, 1915, which displayed a remarkably broad evaluation of Black-Jewish relations, and deserves to be quoted at length. It begins with a specific comparison of the effect of the commercially released film with home movies made at the lynching:

> Exhibitions of moving pictures of the body of Leo Frank as it swung from the limb of a tree near Marietta, Ga., after the mob had done its work, were stopped by the police. This is as it should have been. Any exhibitions that are inflammatory, causing friction between races should be stopped. It is to be hoped that the owners of the 'Birth of a Nation,' who are Jews, will take note of this. Nationality, perhaps, did not enter the minds of the police, but at the same time that race would have felt called on to resent what would have been considered an insult had the exhibitions been permitted.

From here the editorial moves on to a more expansive consideration of the power of moving images and what controls need to be placed upon them in a just society:

> The Jews claim to be very friendly to the Negroes in a way. They say that the races have similarly suffered, and because of that fact they say there should be something of a common cause. They have in mind civil rights, freedom from abuse owing to races. And yet in the face of this we find launched amid us the

most insinuating vehicle of hate known to our race since the days of freedom. The enterprise is defended on the score that it is legitimate; it does not violate the laws; it is peaceful . . . and the rest of it. This is all true, nor [will] we . . . recite the same of a possible Frank picture exhibition. No; they are not decidedly parallel cases. But is there any doubt about the greatest possibly injured persons in either event? (28 Aug. 1915: 4)

There is a very simple and profound demand being made between the lines of this editorial: Jews must begin to walk it like they have been talking it. (Of course an assumption is also being made that "Jew" implies a unified interest group, with no distinction made between, for instance, a social worker and NAACP member such as Lillian Wald and the Jewish capitalists who bought the rights to issue *Birth of a Nation* .) In the ensuing years Jews would certainly begin to ask for similar demonstrations of organized African American faith; in 1924, for instance, Louis Marshall of the American Jewish Committee appealed to the NAACP to stop using the swastika as a "decorative symbol" in their journal, the *Crisis*, because it had already become the emblem of the anti-Semite in Germany (Rosenstock 39).

The conclusion of this compelling editorial leaves no doubt that one way in which Jews and African Americans share common cause is that both groups were still being judged reductively by the actions of extraordinary representatives, for good or bad (and conversely that individuals were being judged by how their behavior affected the race). At a time when leading African Americans were referred to as "race men" and "race women," it is not surprising to uncover a first principle that held that the actions of marginalized people were to be evaluated on the margins where they existed—that is, as racialized behavior. So, the *Freeman* concluded,

> We can't see the good of Julius Rosenwald, that whole-souled Jewish philanthropist, spending his hundreds of thousands in the Y.M.C.A. and educational work, in the hopes of doing general good for the race, if there are other movements that negative him. We advance this from a race viewpoint, thinking that Mr. Rosenwald meant . . . his generosity [to] be associated with his race. He is also conscious of the fact that his race reaps largely from the Negroes. And we cannot deny that there is also a spirit of reciprocity— wherever the Jews are in business in a colored community they do not hesitate in employeing [sic] Negroes to help them. This is so general, and the thing of interdependence is so evident that it is difficult to understand, in connection

with the other conditions already discussed, why Jews would have anything to do with pictures that are so distasteful to the Negroes and so harmful. (28 Aug. 1915: 4)

The circle comes complete here. Each Jew is connected not only to every other Jew but to all of Black America as well. Taking interdependence as a neutral fact, the Indianapolis paper closes with a linkage of rights and responsibilities. This theme would come to function in a sense as the repressed in Black-Jewish relations, returning dramatically again and again, but perhaps most pointedly in the 1930s in discussions surrounding the hiring of African American women to work in Jewish homes (Greenberg 79; Ottley 126–27; Offord). A form is emerging here for talking about "Black-Jewish relations": with intergroup closeness functioning as the norm, any deviation from peaceful coexistence is understood not only as an unfortunate development but indeed as a complete betrayal of authentic racial behavior.

On the same date as the Indianapolis piece, another African American newspaper, the *St. Paul/Minneapolis Appeal*, reached a decidedly less sanguine judgment about Jewish involvement with this movie. This paper did not seize on Jewish backing of *Birth of a Nation* as providing a needed opportunity to renegotiate the terms of the contract between African Americans and Jews but instead read it as a final chapter in an ignominious history: "The fact that three Jews have bought the rights for the state of Massachusetts for the production of 'The Birth of the Nation' [sic], the infamous and false film and that Jewish capitalists are exploiting the photo-play all over the country should cause the colored people to see that many of their most bitter enemies are Jews." This editorial then goes on to list some Jewish "enemies," including leaders of the disenfranchisement movement in Maryland and Julius Rosenwald, whose contribution to the building of a Black Y.M.C.A. was seen as aiding "efforts to segregate" African Americans. The Minnesota newspaper, while admitting that not all Jews were "enemies of the colored people," still found it "queer work for a people who have been oppressed for thousands of years" to take "a special delight in swiping the colored man" (28 Aug. 1915: 2). In the moment of Frank's lynching, Black-Jewish relations had gone national, as these newspaper items attest, but it is obviously misleading to imagine 1915 as the starting point of untroubled alliance.

The most significant point to be made about these editorials on *Birth of a Nation*, I think, comes not from any particular argument contained within them but rather from the very fact of them. Movies were not exempted from these very serious discussions of racial status in the modern world; on the contrary, the motion picture was correctly perceived to be a primary carrier of modernity, with a very real power to move people.[11] As such, African American leaders would have no choice but to confront film and try to attenuate its negative effects, or else risk being defined away as artifacts of a premodern past. It was crucial to remind the white world that "the race" could compete in the modern world and would not stand for being reduced to, and effectively erased by, the minstrel stereotype that Jim Conley's "friends" applied to him or the "bad nigger" tag slapped on by his enemies. These projections would have to give way to a more complex, cosmopolitan image.

Although connections made between *Birth of a Nation* and the Leo Frank case were at times obscure, the appeal of the analogy accents how instrumental this affair had become for a variety of Americans searching for authoritative ways to insert themselves into the principal racial contests of the day. This is nowhere more clear than in examples of how the Frank lynching was adopted by journalists and other public figures looking to score points about American imperialism and colonialism, or to establish positions on the related topic of the responsibility of the "civilized" world to the "savage" world.

A central argument advanced by many editorialists, whether in African American newspapers or general dailies, was that the lynching of Leo Frank brought home the absurdity of the United States' relatively new claim to preeminence in world affairs, especially its self-constructed vision of becoming the world's moral police force. African American papers were particularly likely to seize on the fact of the lynching of a (white) American citizen as evidence of the moral unfitness of the present Democratic administration to serve as moral police even at home. Without shying from the terms of racial *realpolitik*, African American papers welcomed, in one sense, the lynching of a provisional white man: perhaps now more attention would be paid to their calls for federal antilynching legislation.[12] More generally, African American leaders viewed the entire affair as offering them an opportunity to ascend to a moral high ground from which their pronouncements on American culture might have greater resonance than usual. As the *New York Age* put it, "the lynching of Frank has served one great purpose, it has served to fix the eye of the nation upon this bold fact, that Georgia and several of her sister states are not civilized, in the modern sense of the word. And this is something which innumerable lynchings and burnings of colored men, women and children have failed to do" (26 Aug. 1915: 4). The *Amsterdam News* upped the ante by adding a modest proposal: "We might get Africa and other so-called uncivilized countries to send missionaries to civilize the barbarians of Georgia" (qtd. in *Denver Star*, 28 Aug. 1915: 1). Frank's death removed the immediate threat of guilt being shifted onto Jim Conley for Mary Phagan's death, and African American leaders became more willing to forge a temporary symbolic alliance with Jews, against the American system that oppressed them both. But by employing this familiar duality (savage versus civilized) and accepting its implications (the savage must be civilized, or at least managed), this stance validated a kind of rhetoric that African Americans would never be able to activate with the kind of real power it would have when used against them. In other words, this was a clever intellectual gambit, but it existed only on the most rarified level—with no practical way to apply it.

More effective, and less likely to serve dominant interests, were attempts to link Georgia's shame with specific foreign policy concerns. For example, much was made of the seizure of Haiti, which also took place in 1915. There was an incongruity in having an American military presence in Haiti when the troops might be better deployed at home. The *Wichita Beacon* put it most succinctly: "The nation is now in the unique and contradictory attitude of having its marines on the soil of Haiti, and its battleships in front of Port Au Prince, correcting a species of lawlessness that was no greater—if as great—as the lawlessness perpetrated last night in one of the constituent states of its own federation."[13]

But the African American community did not have a unified position on what the role of the United States should be in Haiti. In a prepared statement released by a group of African American leaders, William Monroe Trotter exploited the lynching of Leo Frank to take a swipe at his own rival, Booker T. Washington. African Americans were not "either surprised or shocked" by the violence done Frank, "since lynchings just as fiendish are visited almost daily upon some colored American." Trotter continued by claiming that, given this state of affairs, "all colored people are amazed" that Booker T. Washington had suggested that the United States government make a protectorate out of "the black republic of Hayti, especially under a 'South in the saddle' administration." For the sake of argument Trotter claimed that the band of Marietta men who lynched Frank represented the government of the United States. This government ought to "cease lynching her own colored citizens" before having the gall to dictate the affairs of other countries. This type of isolationism was much different from that preached by the reigning Democrats; it derived not from the self-satisfied anxiety that foreign entanglements could only disturb the precious balance of American life but that foreign policy could not be effectively transacted until the American house was in order.[14] This statement is also remarkable for its erasure of Frank's Jewishness, and of Frank himself as worthy of comment. Lynching was something done to African Americans, even when it was done to a Jew. In other words, Frank's lynching was not allowed to become the special property of Jews but instead was assimilated into African American history in order to advance current political concerns.

While African American papers incorporated the Frank lynching into a history of American racial oppression, mass-circulation papers sympathetic to Frank's cause were quick to place his persecution into a recognizable chronicle of international Jewish suffering. The available model for these editorial writers was the Russian pogrom rather than the history of lynching as it existed in America. Georgia's crime, according to a paper in Erie, Pennsylvania, put "that state on the lowest level of Russian pogroms."[15] Americans of long memory would recall the especially bloody pogrom of 1903 and would understand the reference made by the *Toronto Mail Empire*, which wrote sardonically that the citizenry of Atlanta appeared "to have about the same opinions of Jews as the people of Kishinev."[16] These references are striking for what must be termed either their nearsightedness or their willful refusal to make more homegrown analogies. A non-African American was lynched, and the first line of comparison in America would most obviously be to the group who usually suffered this fate. But this comparison was too uncomfortable — either for Jews who did not want to consider themselves individually so vulnerable, or other whites who were concerned about the slippery-slope nature of such an analogy.

Perhaps one answer to this conundrum might be found in an article written by a Jew for the NAACP's *Crisis* magazine in 1912. In this piece, I. M. Rubinow wrote that one point of comparison between African Americans and Jews is that both were frequently accused of race-specific crimes, "ritual murder in Russia and Rape in America; and each country had its own solution, pogrom in Russia and lynch mob in the United States" (qtd. in Bloom 36–37). But the overall impression conveyed by these analogies is that "Jewish American" was not being affirmed as a recognizable identity. "Jew," as it was being used after Frank's lynching to designate "one who suffers" was applied by the mainstream press to those who lived under Russian tyranny. Since "Negro" was the term usually applied to those who are persecuted in the United States, the African American press was quick to use Frank's death as a springboard for renewed calls for antilynching legislation.

More surprising yet was the resistance to using the Atlanta race riot of 1906 as a corollary.[17] Here in Frank's adopted hometown the slaughter of African Americans had followed on the heels of charges that white women were being victimized sexually. Many Jews were quick to condemn the violence with in-group terminology: one Atlantan called it a "pogrom on the blacks" (qtd. in Hertzberg 191). Hasia Diner has demonstrated that Jews were often quick to compare African American suffering to the persecution of Jews in Russia; in fact, the Frank case would later be "invoked over and over again in articles and editorials condemning violence against black Americans" (43, 98). But to use the experience of African Americans to describe that of Jews in America was resisted. It was safe, after Frank's lynching, to say he was treated as badly as a Jew in Russia would be; it was less attractive for Jews (or even mainstream papers) to admit that a Jew was treated like an African American in Georgia. Earlier on, Leo Frank's mother had been one of the few to make the comparison blatantly; she wrote to her son that she had heard that "the jews are considered not one whit better than negroes in Atlanta."[18]

The trial and tribulations of Leo Frank did, however, lead many observers to note that rampant race prejudice had come to resemble an opportunistic virus, with little motive other than successful attack. In a time of growing nationalism and xenophobia it surprised virtually no one that fresh victims for an age-old bias needed to be procured. The only question left unresolved was whether, as the *Richmond Planet* put it, the "noose slipped this time and caught a white man in its coils" or whether there was a logical necessity at work in the shift from African American to Jewish victim (21 Aug. 1915: 4).[19] The *Jewish Criterion* also concluded, by implication anyway, that Jews were next in line after African Americans as potential lynching victims: "it must follow as the night the day that as yesterday a negro was lynched, what is to prevent a white man from being lynched tomorrow. And if one white man, why not another?"[20] The obvious logic here is that Jews would naturally be the first "whites" to suffer the fate normally reserved for African Americans once the floodgates were opened.[21] If Frank was to be understood in death as a "white man" then the terrors of lynching might be brought home to a wider population; if, instead, his lynching represented only a slight move up the racial chain, then it would not seem as disturbing to the wider public.

Very few commentators constructed a hierarchy of racial victimization around Frank's lynching, and those who did usually read economic competition as the root cause of the violence. The *Elizabeth (N.C.) Independent* offered this analysis: "The Georgia temperament is the product of race hatred and religious bigotry. Back of both is business. It is good business in Georgia to hold the Negro and the Jew, and lately the Roman Catholic in contempt. So long as the landlord and the merchants can keep the Negro down, they can keep the poor white man down; if the landlords and the merchants can keep the Jew down, they can make more business for themselves."[22] New York City's *Call*, a socialist paper, adopted a similar approach with its bid for the United States to "abolish the competitive system," and then watch as "race hatred, in its Atlanta manifestation," dies out.[23]

A more common judgment followed the illness metaphor and viewed the South as if it were a compromised immune system. The fullest statement of this point of view came in an editorial from the *Brooklyn Daily Eagle*: "Lynching is a form of blood bestiality that is derived from slavery days. White men in the South learned this cowardice by attacking negroes at first. Evil becomes increasingly more hideous and uncontrollable. Following the war, white men began to fall by the same process-practice on the cheap lives of the blacks had perfected the art of terror."[24] Similarly, Washington, D.C.'s African American newspaper charged that all along the South had been "sowing only to reap a whirlwind." As the *Bee* put it, the white citizens of the South had been "steeped in crime and immorality" and had now begun "to lynch its own" (28 Aug. 1915: 4). Again, we see how the particularities of Frank's racial and religious identity — so crucial to his original prosecution — are almost completely erased with his death. The *New York Post* put it even more succinctly, worrying that "once the lynching mania is allowed to run unchecked, nobody is safe."[25] Tom Watson was enraged by these attacks on his home state. The suggestion that white Georgians had acted irrationally suggested to Watson that they were tacitly being called Black: Georgia, according to Watson, was being "treated by other states as though we were wooly-headed worshippers" of Voodoo (*Watson's Magazine*, Sept. 1915: 254).

While Frank's lynching was usually lamented, some African American newspapers, in careful language, welcomed Frank's death as providing the attention that might ultimately alleviate their own suffering. The *Chicago Defender* exulted in its belief that because of the outcry caused by Frank's death "the back bone of the mob spirit will forever be crushed and incidentally, the life and liberty of the Afro-Americans in the South will thereby be measurably secured."[26] The general belief that Jewish suffering would eventually result in gains for both Jews and African Americans was to become a familiar theme in the African American press. In 1922, for instance, A. Philip Randolph's *Messenger* welcomed Harvard quotas on Jewish students with this reasoning: "Hitting the Jew is helping the Negro. Why? Negroes have large numbers and small money. Jews have small numbers and large money. Not only that — the Jews control the powerful media for the dissemination of opinion — namely, the press, the screen and the stage" (qtd. in Bloom 82).[27]

Not all of Randolph's contemporaries shared his views on the meaning of Jewish suffering for African American liberation struggles. A notable dissent came from Cyril Briggs, in his nationalist paper, the *Crusader*. In one editorial published in 1920, Jews were held up as a negative example of a weak people, perpetually persecuted. If African Americans wanted an example, this argument ran, they should look toward the Japanese, since "caucasian hatred of the Japanese is distinguishable from caucasian hatred of the Jew and Negro in that the first has none of the scorn of the latter." The *Crusader* concluded its case with a rhetorical question: "Which will we follow? The Jew or the Jap?" (Mar. 1920: 11–12).

But African American commentators on Leo Frank's lynching were much more likely to take a lesson from the Jew's suffering that emphasized a more constructive connection of African Americans and Jews. Randolph codified in his position a hypothesis in development as early as 1915 that held that Jewish activism derived from self-interest might have direct benefits for African Americans. As the Frank case attests, African Americans were willing to accept the temporary oppression of Jews as long as it acted as a necessary precursor to their own successful liberation struggles.

We should not be surprised, then, to find a certain callousness displayed by the *Norfolk Journal and Guide* in the process of scoring a partisan political point: "the lynching of Leo Frank served a good purpose in one respect. It aroused the public conscience which had grown apathetic on the crime of lynching."[28] The *Cleveland Gazette* offered Jim Conley unconditional support and walked a narrow tightrope with their evaluation of the case's ending: "While there has never been any doubt in our mind as to the guilt of Leo M. Frank, and while we have all along resented the contemptible 'sentimental' effort of certain daily newspapers and others to foist the dastardly crime . . . on his forced accomplice . . . we certainly do not endorse the dastardly lynch-murder of Frank. . . . It has, however, served a purpose in calling the attention of the country to a lawless condition that has existed in the South ever since the days of 'reconstruction'" (21 Aug. 1915: 2).[29] Earlier in the year James Weldon Johnson had exhorted readers of the *New York Age* to emulate the Jews, who "have reached the place in this country where people dare not discriminate against them no matter what feelings of prejudice they may have" (28 Jan. 1915: 4).[30] On the other hand, as I have already discussed, David Levering Lewis locates 1915 as the year when powerful German Jews were forced to acknowledge how little their position really meant in the face of American prejudice and resolved to ally with African Americans ("Parallels").

The riddle that exists in the gap between these two positions can, I think, be untangled. Jews, as the *New York Age* correctly observed, had achieved the measure of economic and political power by 1915 that would make it impossible for them to be broadly oppressed through legal mechanisms such as Jim Crow laws. Nor was it likely that the sort of organized violence or threat of violence that terrorized African Americans would be leveled at Jews, Leo Frank notwithstanding. But what the activity around Leo Frank must have taught Jews (which Lewis implies, I think) was that they had assumed wrongly that with the basic rights of American citizenship came the full privileges of whiteness. For this, Jews would have to hurry up and wait: as they eased up on their own claims for inclusion at the highest level of American society, Jewish leaders would discover that working for African American liberation would help them gain access to just that place.

It now seems inevitable that accompanying these ruminations on the status of Jews as Jews, and of Jews relative to African Americans there would come a reevaluation of the melting-pot concept. The image of the melting pot, popularized by Israel Zangwill with his 1908 play of the same name, was ripe for some revision (from all sides) in light of the Frank controversy. We recall that Zangwill's main character had settled in America after barely escaping from a Russian pogrom modeled on Kishinev; to him America offered—primarily through marital amalgamation—the hope of the new race of Americans articulated as early as 1782 by J. Hector St. John de Crèvecoeur in his *Letters from an American Farmer* (Crèvecoeur 39–40; Gleason; Sollors 66–101). It became difficult for virtually anyone to retain the Utopian vision in the light of the murder of Mary Phagan and the lynching of Leo Frank.

Jewish partisans and anti-Semites alike jumped into the fray to reinterpret the melting pot in light of the Frank affair. Three competing conclusions emerged: 1) The melting pot was a lie because those in power would not allow ethnics into it; 2) Even when offered the chance ethnics were rejecting Americanization in favor of retaining the old ways; 3) "Melting pot" really meant an epidemic of rampant race mixing. One Jewish editorialist outlined how fearful this case had made Jews for their safety and standing, organizing his piece around a groaner of a pun: "From the manifestations of prejudice and mob violence it becomes difficult to decide whether the 'Melting Pot' which has been apotheosized in America can any longer retain its significance. The Pelting Pot would perhaps be more to the point inasmuch as certain sects and racial entities are pelted with clock-like regularity even in these free and equal United States."[31]

Aside from its "melting/schmelting" tone of exasperation, this editorial does disclose a real anxiety about how deeply held was the American belief in the melting pot. At least one general-interest newspaper, the *Jamestown (N.Y.) Post* saw in Frank's lynching decisive evidence that mainstream America had no interest in making room for newcomers, or nonwhite old-timers. This condemnation of American bias concluded with the contention that "race hatred is by no means confined to the South, however." This paper noted ruefully the unfair "treatment of the Chinese and Japanese on the Pacific Coast, the widespread feeling against peaceful Italians here at the East," and the final irony, that the "only real American is the red Indian and he has suffered most of all"; a Pennsylvania paper suggested that the South was particularly unwelcoming and noted that it was no wonder "that immigrants avoid that section of the country."[32] Such pessimistic interpretations tempered the overly hopeful notion that the melting pot was stirred by an invisible and benign hand; instead they emphasized how important a role permission played in the working of this model.

While Jews and those sympathetic to the plight of Jews might wonder if permission was to be granted, Tom Watson was busy claiming that the issue was one of will: Jews had been given the chance but had been found wanting. He devised an image that easily matched the "Pelting Pot":

> America is big enough to be "the melting pot" of the Old World, provided the metals melt—otherwise, it isn't.
>
> If the Jew is not to amalgamate and be assimilated; if all the very numerous foreign nationalities that are being moved over into this country are to retain their several languages, customs, flags, holidays, ideas of law, education, government, etc., then the melting pot will fail to fuse into one another, these conflicting elements.
>
> In such a case, the melting pot becomes a huge bomb, loaded with deadly explosives. (*Watson's Magazine*, Sept. 1915: 296)

Watson adopts here a species of ethnic typecasting that had not previously made an appearance in this case but which had entered the American consciousness as early as the 1886 Haymarket riots and would find its fullest flowering with the Sacco-Vanzetti affair of the 1920s: the image of ethnics, particularly the "darker" white ones such as Italians and Jews, as bomb-throwing anarchists.

Finally, there were those who found in the Frank case (and even more in the reactions to it in the northern press) proof that melting-pot enthusiasts were really calling for amalgamation, or were unable to reason clearly because they *were* the products of miscegenation. This sort of reaction came most often in the weeks following the lynching during the time when Georgia was being indicted for the actions of the Marietta criminals. Responding to one wholesale castigation of its state, the *Nicholls (Ga.) Journal* pointed out that the offending editorial was "printed by a contemptable [sic], crack-brain lying heathen JEW . . . in the city of Chicago. . . . where the negro and Jew marry and live together."[33] The *Tribune-Herald* of Rowe, Georgia, adopted a more sardonic tone in explaining why those in the North would never be able to understand the completely defensible denouement of the Frank affair. Unlike the South, home of "the only pure blooded race in the country with the possible exception of . . . New England," the North in general "has been overrun with emigrants from all portions of the globe, necessarily making a mongrel race, incapable of working out those high standards of civilization which are upheld by a purer-blooded and more stable race."[34] These largely irrelevant anxieties about the implications of the Frank case for racial purity did not appear only in the heat of the moment; Harry Golden reports that in 1961 a white supremacist group published a newsletter which claimed that "Frank was part of the conspiracy to 'mongrelize' Southern white womanhood" and that the real goal of the 1954 *Brown v. Board of Education* decision was "to avenge his lynching" (Golden 220).[35] The danger, for this third group of interpreters, was that the melting pot had worked too well.

Talking about Leo Frank, even while he was living, was very often a bait-and-switch maneuver. Foregrounding the case was a handy way to get attention that could then be redirected toward a variety of concerns. After his death, as I have shown, it became simpler to summon up "Leo Frank" without attending too closely to the realities of his existence. This said, I want to turn briefly to one legacy the Frank case left to Black-Jewish relations that had very much indeed to do with the actual body of Leo Frank.

Before appealing to Governor John Slaton for clemency in 1915, Leo Frank had one last hope in the judiciary, a writ of habeas corpus that his lawyers argued in front of the United States Supreme Court. Attorney Louis Marshall of the American Jewish Committee drafted the defense brief, which argued in the main that Frank must be released from prison because he had not been given due process under law; the central contention was that a hostile mob surrounding the trial had made it impossible for Frank to obtain a fair hearing, and that in such cases the federal judiciary must provide relief (Dinnerstein 111–12; Cortner 136–38). Frank lost this appeal, with the majority holding that although "mob domination of the proceedings would constitute a denial of a fair trial," no federal action was necessary as long as the state provides an appropriate "corrective process." Oliver Wendell Holmes Jr., joined by Charles Evans Hughes, wrote an important dissent that argued for a broadening of the federal power "to issue writs of habeas corpus for persons in state custody." "Mob law," wrote Holmes, "does not become due process of law by securing the assent of a terrorized jury" (Cortner 137, 142–43).

This dissent became doctrine in 1923 when Holmes was able to incorporate it into a majority opinion in *Moore v. Dempsey.* In October 1919 a riot broke out in Phillips County, Arkansas, which appears to have been caused mainly by white fears over the formation of an African American farmers' union: rumors had spread that land takeovers and assassinations — a concerted struggle for "social equality" — were being planned. The riots left seven African Americans and three whites dead. Twelve African Americans were sentenced to death for crimes they were alleged to have committed during the riot; confessions were secured through torture, the men had no adequate legal counsel, and some juries deliberated as little as seven minutes (Cortner 8–9, 17–18; Waskow 121–74).

The appeals process in this affair was overseen by the NAACP, which with the case "embarked upon what became the Association's most extensive involvement in constitutional litigation up to that time." The U.S. Supreme Court handed down their favorable decision on February 19, 1923, much to the delight of Louis Marshall, who had been devastated by the ruling in *Frank v. Magnum* (Cortner 1–2, 154). As Walter White recounts in his autobiography, Marshall wrote to him after the decision, with a $100 check for the

NAACP and the satisfied sense that the "stone the builders rejected has now become the cornerstone of the temple." Marshall's original letter actually said nothing about a temple but used instead the phrase "the chief of the corner." According to Richard Cortner, White was probably trying to clarify Marshall's meaning; it seems likely too that he was honoring Frank's memory with his reference to the "temple" — the perfectly appropriate updating of "synagogue" for a Reform Jew like Frank (Cortner 158, 222n12; White 25–26, 52–53). Frank's loss was transformed into victory in *Moore v. Dempsey*, a victory that so impressed Louis Marshall that he began to offer his services to the NAACP. In two later cases in particular, one having to do with restrictive housing covenants and the other with white primaries, Marshall helped secure victories for the NAACP (Cortner 158–59; Diner 129–31).

As long as Frank lived, African Americans and Jews had a hard time seeing their way clear to working together for general legal principles; the case itself could become a starting point for alliance work only after the inconvenient problems raised by the fact of Frank's living body were removed. But even so, the apparently universal meanings gleaned were often more specialized than they appeared. African American commentators tended to so obscure the details of Frank's plight as to erase the functional role his Jewishness played in the drama. And, in the same sense, Jews like Louis Marshall seemed similarly content to underplay the significance of Jewishness: one message (and only one, it should be stressed) of Marshall's work on restrictive housing covenants is that Jewish interests could quietly be served through a defense of the rights of African Americans. Even such a tenuous formal alliance was doomed by the class differences that would continue to separate the masses of African Americans and Jews. By 1977 Louis Marshall's own American Jewish Committee was participating in a much different way when a case of special interest to the African American community was heard before the Supreme Court; in the Bakke case the AJC filed an amicus curiae brief that opposed affirmative action. Now, as when Leo Frank remained alive, a Utopian rhetoric of alliance was rendered unworkable as competing interests of African Americans and Jews — invested and revealed in actual bodies — came to light.

EPILOGUE

Reading Trials, Writing Trials

COLD SNAP HITS OUR TOWN. JEWS, NEGROES SUFFER MOST.
Calvin Trillin

Blacks and Jews Both Ask: Who's The Bigger Victim?
New York Times

The history of Black-Jewish relations in the twentieth century can be fairly summed up by the two pieces of newspaper shorthand above, the first an imaginary headline, the second a real pull-quote. These two scenarios (the second written in the wake of the Crown Heights strife of the early 1990s, which produced at least two martyrs, the "Jew" Yankel Rosenbaum and the "Black" Gavin Cato) taken together point to the central dilemma of Black-Jewish relations: are African Americans and Jews best understood as oppressed partners or oppressed rivals? That question structures the rise-and-fall narrative that has dominated studies of Black-Jewish relations. When African Americans and Jews find common suffering at the heart of their relationship, the "alliance" prospers—and we get progressive labor unions, civil rights movements, and curriculum development. When the two groups compete for victim status we get nationalist hate—the Nation of Islam and the Jewish Defense League, in short. Or so the story goes.

131

I have tried to suggest in this book that the social processes that produce that cultural formation we call "Black-Jewish relations" is made up of the constant shifting of gears—from competitors to colleagues and back again. This dialectic is best observed in moments of crisis—the "trial" suggested in my title—which lay bare the mechanisms of Black-Jewish relations. The strategy of reading "trials" (actual court cases and more diffuse cultural clashes) is the best way to approach Black-Jewish relations because it forces us to understand the subject under discussion as both a thing in itself and as a system of cultural representations. The Frank case proves to be a particularly rich opportunity to study Black-Jewish relations because it reveals how African Americans and Jews were meeting in the modern city *and* because it has been a jumping-off point for so many artistic and rhetorical evaluations of the relationship of African Americans and Jews.

In a wonderful essay entitled "On Imagining Foes, Imagining Friendship," the legal scholar and cultural critic Patricia J. Williams proposes that studying Black-Jewish relations the *right* way can serve to fight against one-dimensional stereotypes of both groups. In this essay, she returns to the Crown Heights riots and wonders how it is that the two major communities involved—Caribbean immigrants and Hasidic Jews—came to be reduced in the popular media to "Blacks and Jews." As Williams puts it, such reductive (and politically reactionary) cultural habits have to be "whittled away by persistently detailed descriptions of lived encounters among live neighbors" (375). Barbara Wittow and Frank Lebow wrote a play about the Frank case in 1967—just about the time many historians see the "grand alliance" of Black-Jewish relations starting to come apart—that tries in an interesting way to get at such "lived encounters." In *Night Witch,* Lebow and Wittow make one major alteration to the cast of characters in an otherwise foursquare work: they marry Jim Conley to Leo Frank's domestic servant. This extrapolation is not "true" to the historical record, but it calls attention in a useful way to the complicated webs that connected the major players in the Frank case.

This strange and obscure play sets a good example by reminding us to take Black-Jewish relations in all its public and private dimensions. In an earlier book about meetings of Jews and African Americans in the world of popular music I recounted an anecdote about the African American composer William

Grant Still, whose wife and daughter both claimed that Jewish composer George Gershwin had stolen the main riff of "I Got Rhythm" from Still; the story spoke to a widely-held concern that the relatively privileged status of certain Jews was affording opportunities to exploit African American cultural possessions. How much deeper the anecdote seems now that I know that Still's wife was Jewish and his daughter Black *and* Jewish (Azoulay 102–3; Melnick, *Right* 56, 225n170).

The readable "trials" of Black-Jewish relations are easily found: from the employment of African American domestic workers by Jews to the challenges faced by Black-Jewish couples and their children (the family created by LeRoi Jones/Amiri Baraka and Hettie Jones would be a good starting place) to the problems that plagued O. J. Simpson's defense team, a new geography of Black-Jewish relations will have to come to terms with challenging questions about race and sexuality. The currents of attraction and repulsion running through the field of Black-Jewish relations have been a source of much discomfort for official players and outside observers; the Frank case is only one example of how the relationship of a Jewish American and an African American could — at least on the level of cultural representation — become drenched in sexualized language and imagery. While my reading of the Frank case and the sexualization of Black-Jewish relations is meant to be neither summary nor defining, it is intended to suggest the myriad ways we might explore anew the relationship of African Americans and Jews. The most available narrative of this association has never, for instance, incorporated "homoeroticism"; in fact, this subject has been assiduously avoided. But to understand better the intensity of the *public* moments of affiliation and rejection that mark this relationship, we need to begin uncovering and analyzing its connection to the secret, private history of Black-Jewish relations. This might lead us to abandon the comforts of the linear "rise and fall" narratives that have heretofore defined this subject, but we might also come to accept, and be well served by the idea that rational public discourse has been only one expressive form of a relationship that has never been simply "good" or "bad."

The Frank case also helps us renegotiate the terms of Black-Jewish relations because it compels us to ask what we mean by "Black" and what we mean by "Jewish"; we cannot hope to create meaningful historical paradigms until we know what it is we are trying to explain. In this New South show trial, "Black" and "Jewish" both had invisible modifiers—"southern" and "northern" respectively. Creating those adjectives was important work, and it was not done primarily by African Americans or Jews. This Black-Jewish relation, like all of them, dwelt in a larger racial system organized and controlled by white people. This trial of Black-Jewish relations could not have existed without Mary Phagan, and it would have looked a lot different without the input of Hugh Dorsey or Tom Watson or John Slaton or William Randolph Hearst (owner of the *Atlanta Georgian*). The Frank case reminds us that putting Black-Jewish relations on trial can help us to see how this relationship is shaped by white people and how it shapes the larger racial discourse of the United States.

The postmodern city continues to host similarly confusing "trials" of Black-Jewish relations. In late 1999, for instance, Jews and African Americans banded together to form the main resistance to a Ku Klux Klan rally in New York City. After scaring off a dozen or so Klan members, the assembled protesters looked around, apparently deciding whom to target next. While some found easy prey in New York City police (the "Blu Klux Klan") it soon became clear that the main event for the rest of the day was going to consist of various street battles between Jews and African Americans. According to one *Village Voice* reporter, the trouble started when a group of Jewish activists confronted African American protesters who were carrying placards implicating Jews in the slave trade. One African American man tried to dismiss all Jewish complaints by asking when was "the last time a bed-sheet cracker hung a mutha-fuckin' Jew from a tree?" After much jockeying back and forth, the fabric of the "fragile black-Jewish political alliance" was unraveling again. With a common enemy no longer it sight, it became impossible for most of the gathered (which included many kinds of Blacks and Jews—including a secular Israeli, a Black Israelite, and so on) to get along. But then, magic: a Klan-sympathizer appeared—a straggler, conjured up by some guardian angel of Black-Jewish relations. In the midst of the Black-Jewish bickering appeared this one lone racist, shouting anti-Black and Puerto Rican slurs and "Heil Hitler." The white racist was promptly kicked, punched, and spat upon by a rainbow coalition of the offended. "For a moment," as the *Village Voice* reporter saw it, "blacks and Jews were allies again" (all citations from Noel). African Americans and Jews certainly cannot rely on the Klan (reborn in 1915 in response to Mary Phagan's murder) to keep them together, but this rally helped many of those gathered to gain some perspective on which "trials" they want to prosecute with the most energy.

NOTES

Since this text relies so heavily on original archival research, I have listed the relevant collections here, along with the abbreviations used for each in my notes. While I have generally followed MLA style for parenthetical notes, I have always cited archival sources in endnotes.

Archives (and Abbreviations for Citations)

AHC   Atlanta History Center — Leo Frank Collection (ms. number 91)
BU   Brandeis University — Leo Frank Collection, Special Collection Department, Brandeis University Libraries
EU   Emory University — Special Collections, Robert W. Woodruff Library
GDAH Georgia Department of Archives and History — John Marshall Slaton Collection (accession number 79–182)

Preface

1. An anonymous poem written about Mary Phagan after the murder was fairly up-front about the choice of villains: "Now, while in that building, / Though virtuous and modest, too, / She was brutally murdered / By the Negro or the Jew." This is cited in Frey and Thompson-Frey (142). Other creative works (most notably Fiddlin' John Carson's songs) would be much less evenhanded, confidently assigning blame to Frank.

2. These privileges, obviously, included employing large numbers of young southerners at extremely low wages.

Chapter 1

1. See, for instance, the detailed information at www.peachstar.gatech.edu/ga-stories/homepg.htm.

2. Eleanor Rivenburgh to Lucille Frank, 16 Oct. 1915, in *BU* 1.

3. This is just a slight overstatement. There are other sources—print and cyber—that continue to make hay out of the Frank case. I have decided not to give full citations for these. Jessie Daniels, in a fuller consideration of these materials, does offer listings.

4. H. T. Williams to Governor John Slaton, 28 Apr. 1915, in *BU* Box 2.

5. See MacLean for more on the relationship of labor and sexuality.

Chapter 2

1. Walter White and others have also noted that the showing of a play based on Thomas Dixon's *Clansman* helped inflame bad feelings (*Man* 8; Williamson 174). For an evocative fictional rendering of the riot see also White's neglected novel *Flight* (esp. 65–66 and 72–76).

2. Quoted in the *Denver Post*, 17 Aug. 1915, in GDAH Box 48a.

3. John Higham notes that in the late 1880s some serious anti-Semitic demonstrations broke out in parts of the lower South "where Jewish supply merchants were common" (92). On the complexities of Jewish life in the South, see Kaganoff and Urofsky, and Evans. If one were interested in exploring violence aimed at "new" immigrants in the South, it might be more productive to study, for example, the Italians of Louisiana than the Jews of Georgia.

4. Reuben Arnold also made the comparison to Beilis in his appeal before Judge Leonard Roan for a new trial (10).

5. Leo Frank to Col. M. J. Yeomans, 9 July 1915, in AHC Box 7.

6. The best scholarly example of this approach is in Diner. Anthologies edited by Hentoff and Salzman are also framed by similar assumptions.

7. For an instructive comparison, see two fine essays on Jack the Ripper, by Walkowitz and Gilman.

Chapter 3

1. This is an overly broad caricature of scapegoat theory, but reasonable facsimiles can be found in Dinnerstein, Golden, and Williamson.

2. At the trial Prosecutor Hugh Dorsey was able to elicit the damaging evidence from Frank's mother that she and Frank's father lived off interest from investments. In response to this admission about Frank's father, Dorsey remarked, "Ah, he's a capitalist, is he?" (qtd. in Golden 153; see also Dinnerstein 33).

3. MacLean certainly understands the connection. She writes that because Jews were associated with "unproductive" finance capital, as well as with the vice trade, they

were ripe as potential villains at this moment. Without going into too much detail, MacLean claims correctly that "fears about changing gender roles and sexual jealousies combined with class hostilities in the anti-Semitism of the Frank case" (492).

4. Louis Marshall of the American Jewish Committee was certainly aware of the dangers of any organized Jewish activity on Frank's behalf; as he put it, he thought it would be "most unfortunate if anything were done in this case from the standpoint of the Jews" (qtd. in Rosenstock 91).

5. One Christian newspaper worried over this strong support for Frank and wondered if "a new race problem is raised by this case—that the Jew is protected while the negro is made the scape-goat" (*Lutheran Observer*, 20 Aug. 1915: 6, in *GDAH* Box 45).

6. Herbert Lasher to Leo Frank, 5 Nov. 1914, in *AHC* Box 1. This type of threat would have had great resonance in post-riot Atlanta: the city's credit rating had been badly hurt in the wake of the 1906 violence (Baker 18).

7. "A Georgian" to Governor John Slaton, 23 June 1915, in *BU* Box 4.

8. Mrs. Henry Ozburn to Governor John Slaton, 22 June 1915, in *BU* Box 4.

9. Gilman has written extensively on the feminization of the Jewish man in *The Jew's Body*; *Freud, Race, and Gender*; and numerous other places (see also Trachtenberg 50; Golden 221).

10. The issue is complicated by the fact that the images that attached to Frank were those more usually ascribed to immigrant eastern European Jews, not assimilated German Jews. While Frank bore many of the marks of the assimilated German Jew, there was enough of the foreignness of the *Ostjuden* to set him apart.

11. For a good introduction to American racial anti-Semitism around the turn of the century, see Singerman. For all of the work done on American anti-Semitism, it is only rarely that scholars have bothered to pay much attention to homegrown forms of racial anti-Semitism.

12. See also the excerpt from Albert Aiken's *The Wolves of New York* (1881) in Selzer (42–43) that describes a Jewish man with ferretlike eyes who constantly rubs his hands together. On the vaudeville Jew more generally, see Dormon and Jenkins.

13. Solicitor-General Dorsey made this point in his summation, cataloging some good Jews (Disraeli, Judah Benjamin) and some bad Jews (a murderer in New York, a "rascally" lawyer), concluding with an attempt to generalize to all people: "these great people are amenable to the same laws as you and I and the black race. They rise to heights sublime, but they sink to depths of degradation" (3–4). On the retouched photo see MacLean 919; Golden 221. Golden also notes (44) that immediately after Frank's arrest, one Atlanta paper printed an obviously retouched photograph of him. Under the caption "Monster," Frank was shown "without glasses, which emphasized the protruding eyeballs" while his lips apparently had been made thicker.

14. Various analyses of the Leo Frank case have rested on very different assumptions about how this question would be answered. In *A Little Girl is Dead* (228), Harry Golden has assumed Frank would not be treated as a white man; the more dominant tendency holds that a German Jew in particular would be considered "white." Linde-

mann states plainly that "Jews were accepted as whites" (209). Robert Seitz Frey and Nancy Thompson-Frey also argue that Frank was "treated as a white man unjustly convicted of a crime 'typically' committed by blacks" (61). As I hope will become clear, my conception of Frank's racial status falls somewhere between these two poles. What I want to stress most of all is that differing economies of racialness competed with each other throughout this case; that is, we do not have to decide whether Frank was *always* considered white, but rather *when* he was assigned that position.

15. Abraham Cahan downplayed the "reckless eyeballing" charges by noting that if Frank did look into the dressing room, it was only to make sure that workers were not loafing (422). On appeal, attorney Reuben Arnold insensitively addressed the peeking charge by asserting, "surely a woman isn't so sacred that you can't ask her to perform her contract as she has agreed to do" (36).

16. J. J. Perry to Leo Frank, 12 May 1915, in *BU* Box 2.

17. Loren Smith to Woodrow Wilson, 26 Apr. 1915, in *BU* Box 2.

18. Along these lines, it is instructive to note how often Conley was referred to as "bestial," a "brute," or "savage" in order to reinscribe this image. See defense attorney Reuben Arnold's summation; also see the *Jewish Ledger* (a New Orleans B'nai B'rith newsletter) on 15 Jan. 1915: 15; and clipping from the *Round Rock (Colo.) Leader,* 28 Aug. 1915, both in *GDAH* Box 45. Finally see Bederman for definitions of "civilization" and "savagery" in this era.

19. Isaac Gibson to Governor John Slaton, 22 Apr. 1915, in *GDAH* Box 35. See, for similar wording, J. Becker to Slaton and the Prison Commission, 12 May 1915, in same location.

20. Clipping from *Manchester Union,* 29 June 1915, in *GDAH* Box 47. See also the *Toronto Mail Empire,* 26 June 1915, in *GDAH* Box 48a, which stated that "the crime was one that strongly resembled many that have been attributed to negroes of the lowest type"; the *San Francisco Argonaut* (quoted in *Los Angeles Tribune* of 7 July 1915) called this "a crime rarely committed by a white man and often committed by colored men." This clipping can be found in the Slaton Scrapbooks, *GDAH* Box 1.

21. Williamson has noted previously some of the interesting connections between the Frank case and this movie (472).

22. Historians have differed somewhat on the issue of how directly related were the lynching of Frank and the revival of the new Klan. See Wade (144–45) for a strong connection of the two.

23. From the commutation hearing before Governor John M. Slaton (12–16 June 1915) 86. This record of the Slaton commutation hearings is available at *EU*. Howard continued by stating that the "perversion itself was a more degrading thing than the actual commission of the rape, because . . . it is like saying that a man has some loathsome disease — he falls the minute you make the charge into a class of condemned persons, he is left without character or standing among decent people."

24. "Commutation," *EU* 148–49. It should be noted that Howard's argument before Slaton represented a change of strategy for Frank's defense; at his original trial his

lawyers spent quite a bit of time throwing into question whether Mary Phagan had been sexually abused at all. On this issue, see MacLean (936–38).

25. I cannot resist recording that Howard attempted to make a distinction between lasciviousness and perversion. Lasciviousness, according to Howard, referred to a general "abnormal, absolutely horrible" habit of being. Perversion, on the other hand, was a specific event when somebody deviated from his or her own norm. Here Howard broke the word down into its Latin roots: "*Peri* around, and *verto* to turn — to turn around — I reverse myself"; then Howard claimed that Frank was only a pervert with Mary Phagan if he deviated from his own usual behavior. And since Dorsey had never come down firmly on whether Frank favored his tongue or nose (and indeed which Conley was claiming Frank used) it was impossible to say whether he had practiced perversion in this case: "Suppose he had a preference by way of the nose, and not by way of the tongue, he is not a pervert unless he has a preference by way of the nose, or if he had a preference by way of the tongue and not by way of the nose, he is not a pervert unless he has a preference by way of the tongue." Whew. For this stunning argument, see "Commutation," *EU* 189.

26. See similarly S. P. Orr's letter to the Georgia State Prison Commission of 26 Apr. 1915, at *BU* Box 5, which held that the violence done to Mary Phagan was "not a white man's crime, and further it is not a Jew's crime. They as a people are almost universally law-abiding."

27. A converse of Dorsey's amplification of class can be found again and again in the discourses surrounding the public alliance building that have come to be known as "Black-Jewish relations." Here, Jews and African Americans have been constrained to accent their racial/historical likeness while deflecting attention from their obvious class differences. For a good analysis of this tendency, see Adolph Reed.

28. Watson's influence in determining Frank's fate is hard to gauge but certainly not inconsiderable. Immediately after Frank's death, Louis Marshall, a leading Jewish attorney, claimed that Watson ought to be held responsible as the murderer (*New York Times*, 18 Aug. 1915: 3).

29. Frank's attorney at the commutation hearing noted that the "queer thing" in the case is that "Conley never does describe an act in any clear and unequivocal way" that indicates what the perversion was supposed to be: "The nearest he comes to it . . . is the time that he testifies that he looked through that transom down into Frank's office and saw Frank on his knees in front of a woman with her clothes up to her hips, and her hands on his shoulders. That is as definite as the testimony is anywhere about it. Well, the minute I read that I said, that doesn't define perversion in this record, in this case." In "Commutation," *EU* 186.

30. From the *Griffin (Ga.) News and Sun*, 30 Aug. 1915, in *GDAH* Box 48a. The issue of teeth marks was reexamined in 1922 by French journalist Pierre Van Paasen, who claimed the "marks on Mary Phagan's head and shoulders did not match the X-rays of Leo Frank's teeth" (qtd. in Kean 239).

31. This anecdote seems to be a bizarre refashioning of the anti-Semitic figure of

the *Judensau,* which Joshua Trachtenberg calls "one of the commonest caricatures of the Jew in the Middle Ages," and which portrays the "sow as the mother feeding her Jewish offspring" (26).

32. Conley also recounted that Frank dismissively referred to Lucille Frank as "that big fat wife of mine" (*Brief of Evidence* at 57).

33. Although Frank's primary lawyers (Luther Rosser, Reuben Arnold, and Herbert Haas) all enjoyed outstanding reputations, most now agree that they did a terrible job defending their man.

34. This song, with instrumental accompaniment by Louis Armstrong and Fletcher Henderson, can be found on the collection *Sissy Man Blues.* For similar examples, hear Lucille Miller's "Kitchen Blues" (1926) on *Country Girls, 1926–1929,* and Memphis Minnie's "Keep on Eatin'" (1938) on *Memphis Minnie: Hoodoo Lady.* This last tells of a man who cannot get enough of the singer's "fried apple pie." Also interesting here is Ida Cox's "I Can't Quit That Man" (on *Big Mamas: Independent Women's Blues,* vol. 2), in which the singer boasts of her man's "modernistic technique" that "makes love complete." Of course, these blues songs did not circulate widely enough to make their coded language comprehensible to most white people.

35. David Roediger also suggests that Chinese immigrants were accused of bringing oral sex into the United States (179). For a complementary discussion of how homosexual practices are labeled with a variety of national names, see Hirschfeld (150–56).

36. "Commutation," *EU* 187.

37. One man wrote to Governor Slaton to ask directly whether it was his belief that Phagan had "lost her virtue before April 26th." He informed Slaton that this "is the construction that many are placing on your statement." Frank A. Doughman to John Slaton, 13 June 1915. On 24 June 1915 Slaton responded to Doughman without really answering the question. Slaton repeated that Conley swore that Phagan "lost her virtue" on April 26, and went on to write that "in my statement I said that in all probability she did not. I made no reference to anything prior to the 26th of April, on which date she was killed." Both letters in GDAH Box 50a.

38. Georgia Reports 141 Georgia 243, *Frank v. State of Georgia,* October Term 1913 at 254.

39. Georgia Reports 141 Georgia 243, *Frank v. State of Georgia,* October Term 1913 at 267.

40. A 1911 labor reform tract anticipated this figuration, suggesting that a woman who entered the work force was entering a "forest haunted by wolves" (qtd. in D'Emilio and Freedman 208).

41. Thanks to Michael Rogin for this suggestion.

42. Marcuse does not argue that capitalists are bearers of subversive sexuality; I am adopting his argument to make the case that Frank's status as a Jewish capitalist and his alleged perversity could easily become mutually supportive in the public mind.

43. On Jews as parasites see Dobkowski (102); Selzer (69); Theweleit (9–12); Handlin (182); Hitler (150, 305); Feingold (142–46); Rosenstock (220).

44. H. L. Williams [?] to Governor John Slaton, 21 June 1915, in *BU* Box 4.

45. On the white slavery scare, see especially Bristow. Ruth Rosen (15) puts the dates at 1911–16; Francesco Cordasco notes that the Jewish presence in white slavery was obvious as early as 1902 (11).

46. Tom Watson also made reference to the Rosenthal case during one of his rants; see the citation in the *New York Times* (18 Aug. 1915: 3); Frank was also quoted as making reference to the case in the same paper (27 Feb. 1914: 3).

47. While the ritual murder charge has had little currency in the United States, it is not hard to imagine, as Mark Thomas Connelly has suggested, how it might become conflated with a more homegrown form, the captivity narrative. Connelly wisely notes that in white slavery narratives, working women are consistently reduced to "girls" in order to avoid the question of their own will altogether (117–18).

48. Clipping from the *Austin Harpoon* (quoting the *Temple Telegram*), June 1915, in GDAH Box 47.

49. Anonymous to Governor John Slaton, 23 June 1915, in BU Box 4.

Chapter 4

1. "Play with" was not a new phrase; as early as 1813 an African American defendant in a rape trial claimed that he had only been "playing with" the alleged victim, and had not raped her (Hamilton 41).

2. Leo Frank to Dr. David Hawkins, 18 May 1915, in BU Box 1.

3. [Signature illegible] to the Prison Commission and Honorable John M. Slaton, 25 May 1915, in GDAH Box 35.

4. Berry Benson's thoughts were self-published in a pamphlet entitled "Five Arguments in the Frank Case," which can be found in AHC Box 7. This quotation can be found on p. 13.

5. Smith's pamphlet, "My Views as to the Death Notes," can be found in GDAH Box 50b. This quotation is on p. 8.

6. Berry Benson, "Five Arguments in the Frank Case" 4, in AHC Box 7. In a classic bit of having one's cake and eating it too, Benson also claimed (on p. 5) that if "Frank dictated these notes he would have said 'pretend'; he never would have thought of 'play like.' Nor would any other white man. It is too childish, too niggery."

7. Anonymous, "The Death Notes——Who is the Mental Author?" in GDAH Box 45.

8. The other two are the use of metaphor and simile and the use of verbal nouns. It is interesting to note that one of the examples Hurston offers of a common double descriptive is "High-tall" (25).

9. William Smith, "My Views as to the Death Notes" 18, in GDAH Box 50b.

10. Clipping from the *Austin Harpoon*, June 1915, in GDAH Box 47.

11. Berry Benson, "Five Arguments in the Frank Case" 2–3, in AHC Box 7. On appeal, Reuben Arnold argued similarly that the notes were "negro" from start to finish, "in thought, in composition, in everything" (51).

12. A. H. Foster to Governor John Slaton, 15 June 1915, in GDAH Box 35. As I

have been discussing it, "Negro" dialect—what it was, who had access to it—became a prominent concern in the Frank case. It should also be noted that Yiddish also surfaced on a few occasions as the Jews' own "secret" language. One of Frank's lawyers warned Lucille Frank not to employ certain Yiddish words in correspondence that might become public. He told her "in the future, do not write on a postal card anything like the word 'muzzumah.' You can not be too careful." Since "muzzumah," according to Leo Rosten (230)—who spells it as "mazuma"—is a vulgarism used to describe money, we can assume that attorney Herbert Haas was most concerned that Mrs. Frank's usage of the term would suggest a connection between this mysterious language of the Jews and their control of money and power. Additionally, according to one recent account of Frank's lynching, when "Frank was asked by his abductors if he wanted to write his wife a note . . . he wrote it in Yiddish, which none of the lynchers could read, [so] the note was burned for fear they might be identified" (*Marietta Journal*, 27 Mar. 1986, in GDAH Box 109). This is the only retelling of the lynching story that I have found that mentions this detail. For the Haas letter, see Herbert Haas to Lucille Frank, 2 Aug. 1915, in AHC Box 5.

13. A study of African American women working in Jewish homes is sorely needed, particularly surrounding the issue of the Bronx Slave Market.

14. On Joel Chandler Harris, see Sundquist 323–47.

15. See also in Dinnerstein (205n56) for Conley's later admission that he wrote the letters, still claiming that someone else must have put the dirty parts in. Annie Maud Carter also swore an affidavit (which she later repudiated in a second one) saying that Conley had confessed to her. In the second affidavit Carter insisted that Frank's lawyers gave her poison to give to Conley.

16. The letters can be found in GDAH Box 35.

17. See Georgia Reports 141 Georgia 243, *Frank v. State of Georgia*, October Term 1913.

18. Berry Benson, "Five Arguments in the Frank Case" 12, in AHC Box 7.

19. The most egregious recent instance of this approach can be found in Benjamin Ginsberg's smug book *Fatal Embrace*. On this, see my essay "Black and Jew Blues."

20. William Smith, "My Views as to the Death Notes" 33–34, in GDAH Box 50b.

Chapter 5

1. And it was not impossible to continue to voice New South boosterism, even in the face of the Frank case. One Georgia paper insisted that "Atlanta and the whole state of Georgia not only have no prejudice against a stranger, but we cordially invite manufacturers and investors, farmers and the better class of immigrants to make their homes and engage in business among us" (*Macon Telegraph*, qtd. in *New York Times*, 5 Mar. 1914: 2). On the other hand, the Jewish leader Cyrus Adler recalled hearing an Arkansas man in 1911 arguing that Jews were generally not wanted in the South because, as he put it, "we already have one race question in Arkansas and that is all we can stand" (qtd. in Rosenstock 88).

2. [Unknown writer] to Lucille Frank, 20 Dec. 1914, in *AHC* Box 1.

3. Mrs. F. G. Fleur to Lucille Frank, 15 Dec. 1914, in *AHC* Box 1. Emphasis in original.

4. A.R.A.F. to Lucille Frank, 15 Dec. 1914, AHC Box 1.

5. Belle Miller to Lucille Frank, 31 May 1915, in *AHC* Box 3.

6. I. P. W. Glenn to Luther Z. Rosser, 2 June 1915, in *BU* Box 3. After Frank's death, one sympathizer wrote to the Milledgeville State Prison warden to tell him that Frank had communicated his innocence from beyond the grave. This man said that he received a communication from Frank through a trumpet medium: Frank told him he was "entirely innocent of the murder of Mary Phagan" but still wanted to thank "each and every one of the mob" who lynched him for "liberating his real self." According to this man, Frank also said that he had been in touch with Mary Phagan, who told him who was really responsible for the crime; for the present, however, Frank did not want to "divulge the names of the parties" except to note that they both worked in the factory. See R.L.M. to Warden, Milledgeville State Prison, 22 Aug. 1915, in *AHC*, Box 7.

7. I think this might be related to a tendency for newspapers that were unsympathetic to Frank to refer to his defenders as "sentimental." See, for instance, the *Cleveland Gazette*, 21 Aug. 1915: 2. In a similar vein, the *Cahnute (Kans.) Tribune* wrote that "there is considerable mushy flapdoodle being smeared on the landscape" as a result of Frank's lynching. For this clipping see *GDAH* Box 45.

8. And the automobile would finally make a significant appearance in this affair as well; Frank's lynching has been called the first ever in which automobiles played an important role (Golden 291).

9. The most interesting of the earlier references I have found came in the *Savannah Tribune* in May 1915. This paper compared the release of *Birth of a Nation* to a biopic that Hal Reid, a supporter of Frank, had made to encourage public sentiment in favor of him. The *Tribune* began by noting that successful fights had been made to prohibit showings of Griffith's movie; this article goes on to argue that anything "that would inflame the minds of the public against any race or class of people should not be allowed to be presented publicly." The *Tribune* then makes an argument about the social meaning of the release of the Frank film: "This is being done in order to manufacture sentiment favorable to the condemned murderer. This, too, is being done at the expense of the colored man who figured prominently in the case." Film, it was beginning to appear, was a medium generally unfriendly to the concerns of African Americans (*Savannah Tribune*, 22 May 1915: 2).

10. Clipping from *Boston Evening Herald*, 21 Aug. 1915, in *GDAH* Box 48a.

11. An African American newspaper, the *Cleveland Gazette*, quoted a white paper that suggested quite pointedly that the South no longer be allowed "to propagandize its doctrine of race-hatred, anarchy and blood-lust throughout the land by means of lying novels and motion pictures" (28 Aug. 1915: 2).

12. Arnold Shankman has recorded very similar reactions from African American papers after the lynching of eleven Italians in New Orleans in 1891 (86–87).

13. Clipping from the *Wichita Beacon*, 17 Aug. 1915, in *GDAH* Box 45.

14. For the Trotter quotations, see clipping from the *Boston Evening Herald*, 21 Aug. 1915, in GDAH Box 48a.

15. Clipping from *Erie (Penn.) Times*, 18 Aug. 1915, in GDAH Box 45.

16. Clipping from the *Toronto Mail Empire*, 26 June 1915, in GDAH Box 48a. One paper even noted sarcastically that "Georgia can give Russia cards and spades on elegance of organization for a pogrom. High powered automobiles and prominent citizens beat cossack pony riders and riff raff citizenry afoot for style" (*Washington [Penn.] Observer*, 18 Aug. 1915, in GDAH Box 45). Similarly, one Jewish paper, making reference to the Beilis blood-libel case, mentioned that "even the vodka besotted moujiks respected the verdict" of that court (*Jewish Independent*, 28 Aug. 1915: 1).

17. The *St. Paul/Minneapolis Appeal* is the only paper I have found which made mention of the Atlanta riot (25 Sept. 1915: 2).

18. Mrs. Rae Frank to Leo Frank, no date, in AHC Box 1. The *Brooklyn Daily Eagle* argued similarly that Frank would have been safe from persecution had he been a "white man" (19 Aug. 1915, clipping in GDAH Box 45). Also see the *Washington Bee* (21 Aug. 1915: 4), which argues that the "Jew has no more rights that Southern oligarchy respects than a colored American."

19. Earlier that summer the *Planet* wrote similarly that the "prejudice of years against the Negro is now asserting itself against the white man" (25 June 1915: 4). On a related note, one racist journal suggested that somehow African Americans were to blame for all of this strife anyway: according to the *World's Work*, the presence of the Negro in the South "pulled down the standards of the white population," which led to all sorts of mayhem (Oct. 1915: 637–38).

20. Clipping from the *Jewish Criterion*, 20 Aug. 1915, in GDAH Box 45.

21. Of course we should recall that this simply was not so. In 1891, as I have mentioned previously, eleven Italians were lynched in New Orleans, following the murder of the superintendent of police there (Higham 91). And as a corrective to all this hand wringing, James Weldon Johnson reminded readers of the *New York Age* that "there is no prejudice against Jew or Gentile, Greek or barbarian, Buddhist or Mohamedan, Chinaman or the South Sea Islander, that would equal the prejudice against an American Negro" (*New York Age*, 3 June 1915: 4).

22. Clipping from the *Elizabeth City (N.C.) Independent*, 19 Aug. 1915, in GDAH Box 48a. The *Hutchinson (Kans.) News* (clipping from 18 Aug. 1915, in GDAH Box 45) took the same approach: "It is difficult for the people of the United States, generally, to understand the feeling that exists in the South, especially, and in Georgia, probably more than any other state, against the Hebrew. It amounts to far more than the feeling against the negro, and there is no foundation for it, save trade . . . He has taken the trade of the cities from the Southerner and the feeling against the Hebrew race is intense."

23. Clipping from the *Call*, 28 June 1915, in GDAH Box 1 (Slaton Scrapbooks).

24. Clipping from the *Brooklyn Daily Eagle*, 19 Aug. 1915, in GDAH Box 45.

25. Clipping from the *New York Post*, no date, in GDAH Box 45.

26. Quoted in clipping from the *Great Falls (Mont.) Tribune*, 28 Aug. 1915, in GDAH Box 48a.

27. A related sentiment was voiced in the *New York Age* (13 May 1915: 4), in an unsigned editorial that endorsed Jacob Schiff's call for 2,000,000 more Jews to immigrate to America and settle west of the Mississippi: "If 2,000,000 more Jews settle in this country it will eventually be the cause of bettering conditions for the Negro."

28. Clipping from the *Norfolk Journal and Guide* (28 Aug. 1915), in the Tuskegee Institute Archives, News Clipping File, Reel 221, Frame 161.

29. *Cleveland Gazette*, 21 Aug. 1915: 2. For a summary of this type of reaction, see Levy (218). Even Booker T. Washington carefully expressed his wish that this crime would "arouse Georgia against every form of lawlessness." Quoted in clipping from the *Boston Herald*, 18 Aug. 1915, in GDAH Box 48a.

30. A month later the *Age* added that "of course, we have not the wealth of the Jews, but there is no reason why we should not be just as effectively organized" (25 Feb. 1915: 4).

31. Clipping from the *Jewish Criterion*, 20 Aug. 1915, in GDAH Box 45.

32. Clipping from the *Jamestown (N.Y.) Post*, no date, in GDAH Box 45; clipping from the *Columbia (Penn.) Sky*, no date, in GDAH Box 45.

33. Clipping from the *Nicholls (Ga.) Journal*, 27 Aug. 1915, in GDAH Box 48a.

34. Clipping from the *Rowe (Ga.) Tribune-Herald*, 31 Aug. 1915, in GDAH Box 48a.

35. This publication, known as *Thunderbolt: The White Man's Viewpoint*, was the organ of the National States Rights Party of Birmingham. An earlier conspiracy theorist suggested that Woodrow Wilson might appoint Louis Brandeis, a Jew, to the Supreme Court, to make up for his "failure to act in the Frank case" (*Ogden [Utah] Examiner*, 29 Jan. 1916, in GDAH Box 48b).

WORKS CITED

Daily newspaper articles are cited in the text only by date; more extensive reviews and magazine articles are cited separately by title in the list below. Obvious typographic errors from these sources have been silently corrected. Many of the African American newspapers cited in this book were found in the Tuskegee Institute Archives News Clipping File.

Legal Sources

Brief of the Evidence, Leo M. Frank v. State of Georgia, Fulton County Superior Court at the July Term, 1913
Georgia Reports 141 Georgia 243, Frank v. State of Georgia, October Term, 1913

Magazines/Newspapers

Atlanta Constitution
Cleveland Gazette
Crusader
Denver Star
Indianapolis Freeman
Jeffersonian
Jewish Independent (Cleveland)
New York Age

New York Times
Richmond Planet
Savannah Tribune
St. Paul/Minneapolis Appeal
Washington (D.C.) Bee
Watson's Magazine
World's Work

Internet Source

www.peachstar.gatech.edu/ga-stories/homepg.htm

Books, Articles, and Other Sources

Addams, Jane. *A New Conscience and an Ancient Evil*. New York: MacMillan, 1914.

Arnold, Reuben R. *The Trial of Leo Frank (Reuben R. Arnold's Address to the Court in His Behalf)*. Intro. by Alvin V. Sellers. Baxley, Ga.: Classic, 1915.

Azoulay, Katya Gibel. *Black, Jewish, and Interracial: It's Not the Color of Your Skin, But the Race of Your Kin and Other Myths of Identity*. Durham, N.C.: Duke University Press, 1997.

Baker, Ray Stannard. *Following the Color Line: An Account of Negro Citizenship in the American Democracy*. 1908. Williamstown, Mass.: Corner House, 1973.

Batteau, Allen W. *The Invention of Appalachia*. Tuscon: University of Arizona Press, 1990.

Becker, Howard S. *Outsiders: Studies of the Psychology of Deviance*. London: Free Press, 1963.

Bederman, Gail. *Manliness and Civilization: A Cultural History of Gender and Race in the United States, 1880–1917*. Chicago: University of Chicago Press, 1995.

Berson, Lenora E. *The Negroes and the Jews*. New York: Random House, 1971.

Big Mamas: Independent Women's Blues. Vol. 2. Rosetta Records, 1982.

Bingham, Theodore A. "Foreign Criminals in New York." *North American Review* 188.3 (Sept. 1908): 383–94.

Birken, Lawrence. *Consuming Desire: Sexual Science and the Emergence of a Culture of Abundance, 1871–1914*. Ithaca, N.Y.: Cornell University Press, 1988.

Bloom, Steven. "Interactions Between Blacks and Jews in New York City, 1900–1930, as Reflected in the Black Press." Diss., New York University, 1973.

Bogle, Donald. *Toms, Coons, Mulattoes, Mammies, and Bucks: An Interpretive History of Blacks in American Film*. 1973. New York: Continuum, 1989.

Bristow, Edward J. *Prostitution and Prejudice: The Jewish Fight Against White Slavery, 1870–1939*. Oxford: Clarendon, 1982.

Brundage, W. Fitzhugh. *Lynching in the New South: Georgia and Virginia, 1880–1930*. Chicago: University of Illinois Press, 1993.

Bullough, Vern L. *Sexual Variance in Society and History*. Chicago: University of Chicago Press, 1976.

Busch, Francis X. *Guilty or Not Guilty?* London: Arco, 1957.

Cahan, Abraham. *Bleter Fun Mayn Lebn.* Vol. 5. New York: Forward Association, 1931.

Cliff, Michele. *Free Enterprise.* 1993. New York: Plume, 1994.

Cohen, Stanley. *Folk Devils and Moral Panics: The Creation of the Mods and Rockers.* 1972. Oxford: Martin Robertson, 1980.

Connelly, Mark Thomas. *The Response to Prostitution in the Progressive Era.* Chapel Hill: University of North Carolina Press, 1980.

Connolly, C. P. *The Truth About the Frank Case.* New York: Vail-Ballou, 1915.

Cordasco, Francesco, with Thomas Monroe Pitkin. *The White Slave Trade and the Immigrants: A Chapter in American Social History.* Detroit: Blaine Ethridge, 1981.

Cortner, Richard C. *A Mob Intent on Death: The NAACP and the Arkansas Riot Cases.* Middletown, Conn.: Wesleyan University Press, 1988.

Country Girls, 1926–1929. Matchbox, 1984.

Crèvecoeur, J. Hector St. John de. *Letters from an American Farmer.* 1782. New York: Dutton, 1957.

Crowe, Charles. "Racial Massacre in Atlanta, September 22, 1906." *Journal of Negro History* 54.2 (1969): 150–73.

———. "Racial Violence and Social Reform Origins of the Atlanta Riot of 1906." *Journal of Negro History* 53.3 (1968): 234–56.

Daniels, Jessie. *White Lies: Race, Class, Gender and Sexuality in White Supremacist Discourse.* New York: Routledge, 1997.

D'Emilio, John, and Estelle B. Freedman. *Intimate Matters: A History of Sexuality in America.* New York: Harper and Row, 1988.

Denning, Michael. *Mechanic Accents: Dime Novels and Working-Class America.* New York: Verso, 1987.

Dershowitz, Alan. "Mob Justice." *Boston Magazine* 89.9 (Sept. 1997): 128–30.

Diner, Hasia R. *In The Almost Promised Land: American Jews and Blacks, 1915–1935.* Westport, Conn.: Greenwood, 1977.

Dinnerstein, Leonard. *The Leo Frank Case.* New York: Columbia University Press, 1968.

Dittmer, John. *Black Georgia in the Progressive Era, 1900–1920.* Chicago: University of Illinois Press, 1977.

Dobkowski, Michael N. *The Tarnished Dream: The Basis of American Anti-Semitism.* Westport, Conn.: Greenwood, 1979.

Dollimore, Jonathan. *Sexual Dissidence: Augustine to Wilde, Freud to Foucault.* Oxford: Clarendon, 1991.

Dormon, James H. "American Popular Culture and the New Immigration Ethnics: The Vaudeville Stage and the Process of Ethnic Ascription." *Amerikastudien* 36.2 (1991): 179–93.

[Dorsey, Hugh M.] *Argument of Hugh M. Dorsey Solicitor-General, Atlanta Judicial Circuit At the Trial of Leo M. Frank, Charged with the Murder of Mary Phagan.* Macon, Ga.: N. Christophulos, n.d.

Dorson, Richard, ed. *American Negro Folktales.* 1956. Greenwich, Conn.: Fawcett, 1967.

Doyle, Don. *New Men, New Cities, New South: Atlanta, Nashville, Charleston, Mobile, 1860–1910.* Chapel Hill: University of North Carolina Press, 1990.

Dyer, Richard. *Heavenly Bodies: Film Stars and Society.* London: BFI-MacMillan, 1986.

Edmundson, Mark. *Nightmare on Main Street: Angels, Sadomasochism, and the Culture of Gothic.* Cambridge: Harvard University Press, 1997.

Ellis, Havelock. *Studies in the Psychology of Sex.* Vol. 4. Philadelphia: F.A. Davis, 1914.

Ellis, Julie. *The Hampton Women.* New York: Simon and Schuster, 1980.

Englestein, Laura. "Morality and the Wooden Spoon: Russian Doctors View Syphilis, Social Class, and Sexual Behavior, 1890–1905." In *The Making of the Modern Body: Sexuality and Society in the Nineteenth Century.* Ed. Catherine Gallagher and Thomas Laquer, 169–208. Berkeley and Los Angeles: University of California Press, 1987.

Erikson, Kai T. *Wayward Puritans: A Study in the Sociology of Deviance.* New York: John Wiley and Sons, 1966.

Evans, Eli N. *The Provincials: A Personal History of Jews in the South.* 1973. New York: Atheneum, 1976.

Fanon, Frantz. *Black Skin, White Masks.* Trans. Charles Lam Markmann. 1952. New York: Grove Weidenfeld, 1967.

Feingold, Henry L. *Zion in America: The Jewish Experience from Colonial Times to the Present.* 1974. Rev. ed., New York: Hippocrene, 1981.

Fiedler, Leslie. "Some Jewish Pop Art Heroes." In vol. 2 of *The Collected Essays of Leslie Fiedler,* 134–40. New York: Stein and Day, 1971.

Fishkin, Shelley Fisher. *Was Huck Black?: Mark Twain and African-American Voices.* New York: Oxford University Press, 1993.

Foucault, Michel. *The History of Sexuality: An Introduction.* 1978. Volume 1 of *The History of Sexuality.* Trans. Robert Hurley. New York: Vintage, 1980.

Frey, Robert Seitz, and Nancy Thompson-Frey. *The Silent and the Damned: The Murder of Mary Phagan and the Lynching of Leo Frank.* New York: Madison, 1988.

Fredrickson, George M. *The Black Image in the White Mind: The Debate on Afro-American Character and Destiny, 1817–1914.* New York: Harper and Row, 1971.

Freedman, Samuel. "Never Forget." *Salon Magazine* (www.salon.com) 12 January 1999.

Freshman, Clark. "Beyond Pontius Pilate and Judge Lynch: The Pardoning Power in Theory and Practice as Illustrated in the Leo Frank Case." Senior honors thesis, Harvard College, 1986.

Freud, Sigmund. *Three Essays on the Theory of Sexuality.* 1905. Trans. James Strachey. New York: Avon, 1965.

Friedman, Lester. *Hollywood's Image of the Jew.* New York: Frederick Ungar, 1982.

Fry, Gladys-Marie. *Night Riders in Black Folk History.* 1975. Athens: University of Georgia Press, 1991.

Gabler, Neal. *An Empire of Their Own: How the Jews Invented Hollywood.* New York: Crown, 1981.

Gagnon, J. H., and W. Simon. "Sexual Conduct: The Social Sources of Human Sexuality" [1973]. In *Human Sexual Relations.* Ed. Mike Brake, 197–222. New York: Pantheon, 1982.

Garber, Marjorie. *Vested Interests: Cross-Dressing and Cultural Anxiety*. New York: Routledge, 1992.

Giles, Patrick. "The Old Religion." *New York Times Book Review* 18 Dec. 1998: 17.

Gilman, Sander. *Freud, Race, and Gender*. Princeton: Princeton University Press, 1993.

———. "'I'm Down on Whores': Race and Gender in Victorian London." In *The Anatomy of Racism*. Ed. David Theo Goldberg, 146–70. Minneapolis: University of Minnesota Press, 1990.

———. *The Jew's Body*. New York: Routledge, 1991.

Ginsberg, Benjamin. *The Fatal Embrace: Jews and the State*. Chicago: University of Chicago Press, 1993.

Girard, Rene. *The Scapegoat*. Trans. Yvonne Freccero. Baltimore: Johns Hopkins University Press, 1986.

———. *Violence and the Sacred*. 1972. Trans. Patrick Gregory. Baltimore: Johns Hopkins University Press, 1977.

Gleason, Philip. "The Melting Pot: Symbol of Fusion or Confusion?" *American Quarterly* 16.1 (1964): 20–46.

Golden, Harry. *A Little Girl is Dead*. New York: World, 1965.

Goren, Arthur A. *New York Jews and the Quest for Community: The Kehillah Experiment, 1908–1922*. New York: Columbia University Press, 1970.

Grady, Henry Woodfin. *The New South and Other Addresses*. New York: Haskell House, 1969.

Greenberg, Cheryl Lynn. *"Or Does It Explode?": Black Harlem in the Great Depression*. New York: Oxford University Press, 1991.

Greene, Ward. *Death in the Deep South*. New York: American Mercury, 1938.

Hall, Jacquelyn Dowd. "Private Eyes, Public Women: Images of Class and Sex in the Urban South, Atlanta, Georgia, 1913–1915." In *Work Engendered: Toward a New History of American Labor*. Ed. Ava Baron, 243–72. Ithaca: Cornell University Press, 1991.

———. *Revolt Against Chivalry: Jesse Daniel Ames and the Women's Campaign Against Lynching*. New York: Columbia University Press, 1979.

Halttunen, Karen. *Murder Most Foul: The Killer and the American Gothic Imagination*. Cambridge: Harvard University Press, 1998.

Hamilton, Marybeth. "'The Life of a Citizen in the Hands of a Woman': Sexual Assault in New York City, 1790–1820." In *Passion and Power: Sexuality in History*. Ed. Kathy Peiss and Christina Simmons, with Robert Padgug, 35–56. Philadelphia: Temple University Press, 1989.

Handlin, Oscar. *Adventure in Freedom: Three Hundred Years of Jewish Life in America*. New York: McGraw-Hill, 1954.

Harlan, Louis R. *Booker T. Washington: The Wizard of Tuskegee, 1901–1915*. New York: Oxford University Press, 1983.

Hentoff, Nat, ed. *Black Anti-Semitism and Jewish Racism*. 1969. New York: Schocken, 1970.

Hertzberg, Steven. *Strangers Within the Gate City: The Jews of Atlanta, 1845–1915*. Philadelphia: Jewish Publication Society of America, 1978.

Higham, John. *Strangers in the Land: Patterns of American Nativism, 1860–1925*. 1955. New York: Atheneum, 1977.

Hirschfeld, Magnus. *Racism*. Trans. and ed. Eden Paul and Cedar Paul. Port Washington, N.Y.: Kennikat, 1938.

Hitler, Adolf. *Mein Kampf*. 1925. Trans. Ralph Manheim. Boston: Houghton Mifflin, 1943.

Hughes, Langston, and Arna Bontemps, ed. *The Book of Negro Folklore*. New York: Dodd, Mead, 1958.

Hurston, Zora Neale. "Characteristics of Negro Expression." In *Negro: An Anthology*. 1933. Collected and ed. Nancy Cunard, abridged by Hugh Ford, 23–31. New York: Frederick Ungar, 1970.

JanMohammed, Abdul R. "Sexuality on/of the Racial Border: Foucault, Wright, and the Articulation of 'Racialized Sexuality.'" In *Discourses of Sexuality: From Aristotle to AIDS*. Ed. Domna C. Stanton, 94–116. Ann Arbor: University of Michigan Press, 1992.

Jenkins, Henry. *What Made Pistachio Nuts?: Early Sound Comedy and the Vaudeville Aesthetic*. New York: Columbia University Press, 1992.

Kaganoff, Nathan M., and Melvin I. Urofsky, eds. *"Turn to the South": Essays on Southern Jewry*. Charlottesville: University of Virginia Press, 1979.

Kauffman, Reginald. *The House of Bondage*. New York: Moffat, Yard, 1910.

Kazin, Alfred. "Oy Gevalt!" *New Republic* 217.18 (3 Nov. 1997): 36–38.

Kean, Mary Phagan. *The Murder of Little Mary Phagan*. Far Hills, N.J.: New Horizon, 1987.

Kinsey, Alfred, Wardell B. Pomeroy, and Clyde E. Martin. *Sexual Behavior in the Human Male*. Philadelphia: W. B. Saunders, 1948.

Kluger, Richard. *Members of the Tribe*. 1977. New York: Bantam, 1978.

Knight, Lucian Lamar. *A Standard History of Georgia and Georgians*. Vol. 2. New York: Lewis, 1917.

Laquer, Thomas W. "Sexual Desire and the Market Economy During the Industrial Revolution." In *Discourses of Sexuality: From Aristotle to AIDS*. Ed. Domna C. Stanton, 185–215. Ann Arbor: University of Michigan Press, 1992.

Lebow, Barbara, and Frank Wittow. "Night Witch." Unpublished ms., ca. 1967.

Levy, Eugene. "'Is the Jew a White Man?': Press Reaction to the Leo Frank Case, 1913–1915." *Phylon* 35.2 (1974): 212–22.

Lewis, David Levering. "Parallels and Divergences: Assimilationist Strategies of Afro-American and Jewish Elites from 1910 to the Early 1930s." *Journal of American History* 71.3 (1984): 543–64.

———. *W. E. B. Du Bois: Biography of a Race, 1868–1919*. New York: Henry Holt, 1993.

Lhamon, W. T. *Raising Cain: Blackface Performance from Jim Crow to Hip Hop*. Cambridge: Harvard University Press, 1998.

Lindemann, Albert S. *The Jew Accused: Three Anti-Semitic Affairs (Dreyfus, Beilis, Frank), 1894–1915*. New York: Cambridge University Press, 1991.

Lott, Eric. *Love and Theft: Blackface Minstrelsy and the American Working Class*. New York: Oxford University Press, 1993.

MacLean, Nancy. "The Leo Frank Case Reconsidered: Gender and Sexual Politics in the Making of Reactionary Populism." *Journal of American History* 78.3 (1991): 917–48.

Malone, Bill C. *Singing Cowboys and Musical Mountaineers: Southern Culture and the Roots of Country Music*. Athens: University of Georgia Press, 1993.

Mamet, David. *The Old Religion*. New York: Free Press, 1997.

Marcuse, Herbert. *Eros and Civilization: A Philosophical Inquiry Into Freud*. 1955. New York: Vintage, 1962.

Matthews, John Michael. "Studies in Race Relations in Georgia, 1890–1930." Diss., Duke University, 1970.

Melnick, Jeffrey. "Black and Jew Blues." *Transition* 62 (1993): 106–21.

———. *A Right to Sing the Blues: African Americans, Jews, and American Popular Song*. Cambridge: Harvard University Press, 1999.

Memphis Minnie. *Hoodoo Lady (1933–1937)*. Columbia Legacy, 1991.

Moore, Deborah Dash. *At Home in America: Second Generation New York Jews*. New York: Columbia University Press, 1981.

———. "Separate Paths: Blacks and Jews in the Twentieth-Century South." In *Struggles in the Promised Land: Toward a History of Black-Jewish Relations*. Ed. Jack Salzman and Cornel West, 275–93. New York: Oxford University Press, 1997.

Murder in Harlem. Dir. Oscar Micheaux. 1935.

The Murder of Mary Phagan. NBC-TV miniseries. Dir. Billy Hale, 1987.

Newby, I. A. *Jim Crow's Defense: Anti-Negro Thought in America, 1900–1930*. Westport, Conn.: Greenwood, 1965.

Noel, Peter. "The Hate that Hate Produced: Inside the Black and Jewish Fight Clubs at the Anti-KKK Rally." *Village Voice* 27 Oct.–2 Nov. 1999. Online: www.villagevoice.com.

Offord, Carl Ruthven. *The White Face*. 1943. New York: AMS, 1975.

Oney, Steve. "The Lynching of Leo Frank." *Esquire* 104.3 (Sept. 1985): 90–104.

Ottley, Roi. *"New World a-Coming": Inside Black America*. Boston: Houghton Mifflin, 1943.

Padgug, Robert A. "Sexual Matters: On Conceptualizing Sexuality in History." In *Passion and Power: Sexuality in History*. Ed. Kathy Peiss and Christina Simmons, with Robert A. Padgug, 14–31. Philadelphia: Temple University Press, 1989.

Parade. RCA Victor, 1999.

Peiss, Kathy. "'Charity Girls and City Pleasures': Historical Notes on Working-Class Sexuality, 1880–1920." In *Passion and Power: Sexuality in History*. Ed. Kathy Peiss and Christina Simmons, with Robert A. Padgug, 57–69. Philadelphia: Temple University Press, 1989.

Reed, Adolph L., Jr. "Blacks and Jews in the Democratic Coalition." In *The Jesse Jackson Phenomenon: The Crisis of Purpose in Afro-American Politics*. New Haven: Yale University Press, 1986.

Reed, Ishmael. "The 'Liberal' in Us All." In *Shrovetide in Old New Orleans*, 37–43. 1978. New York: Atheneum, 1989.

———. *Reckless Eyeballing.* 1986. New York: Atheneum, 1988.

———. "300 Years of 1984." In *Writin' is Fightin': Thirty-Seven Years of Boxing on Paper*, 59–75. 1988. New York: Atheneum, 1990.

Rodgers, Daniel T. *The Work Ethic in Industrial America, 1850–1920.* 1974. Chicago: University of Chicago Press, 1978.

Roe, Clifford G. *Panders and Their White Slaves.* New York: Fleming H. Revell, 1910.

Roediger, David. *The Wages of Whiteness: Race and the Making of the American Working Class.* New York: Verso, 1991.

Rogin, Michael. "'The Sword Became a Flashing Vision': D. W. Griffith's *The Birth of a Nation*." In *The New American Studies: Essays from* Representations. Ed. Philip Fisher, 346–91. Berkeley: University of California Press, 1991.

Rosen, Ruth. *The Lost Sisterhood: Prostitution in America, 1900–1918.* 1982. Baltimore: Johns Hopkins University Press, 1985.

Rosenstock, Morton. *Louis Marshall: Defender of Jewish Rights.* Detroit: Wayne State University Press, 1965.

Ross, Edward A. *The Old World in the New: The Significance of Past and Present Immigration to the American People.* New York: Century, 1914.

Rosten, Leo. *The Joys of Yiddish.* New York: Washington Square, 1968.

Rubin, Rachel. "Sing Me Back Home: Nostalgia, Bakersfield, and Modern Country Music." In *American Popular Music: New Approaches to the Twentieth Century.* Eds. Rachel Rubin and Jeffrey Melnick. Amherst: University of Massachusetts Press, 2000.

Salzman, Jack, ed., with Adina Back and Gretchen Sullivan Sorin. *Bridges and Boundaries: African Americans and American Jews.* New York: George Braziller with the Jewish Museum, 1992.

Samuels, Charles, and Louise Samuels. *Night Fell on Georgia.* New York: Dell, 1956

Schur, Edwin M. *Labelling Deviant Behavior: Its Sociological Implications.* New York: Harper and Row, 1971.

Selzer, Michael, ed. *"Kike!"* New York: Meridian-World, 1972.

Shankman, Arnold. *Ambivalent Friends: Afro-Americans View the Immigrant.* Westport, Conn.: Greenwood, 1982.

Siebel, H. Dieter. "Social Deviance in Comparative Perspective." In *Theoretical Perspectives on Deviance.* Ed. Robert A. Scott and Jack D. Douglas, 251–81. New York: Basic, 1972.

Silber, Nina. *The Romance of Reunion: Northerners and the South, 1865–1900.* Chapel Hill: University of North Carolina Press, 1993.

Simpson, Josselyn, ed. *The Lincoln Center Review.* New York: Lincoln Center, 1998.

Singerman, Robert. "The Jew as Racial Alien: The Genetic Component of American Anti-Semitism." In *Anti-Semitism in American History.* Ed. David A. Gerber, 103–28. Chicago: University of Illinois Press, 1987.

Sissy Man Blues: 25 Authentic Straight and Gay Blues and Jazz Vocals. Jass, 1989.

Smith, Sid. "'Pegasus' 'Lynching of Leo Frank' Revives Issue of Black-Jewish Relations.'" *Chicago Tribune Arts Watch.* 11 Nov. 1998. Online: www.nrstg2s.djnr.com.

Sollors, Werner. *Beyond Ethnicity: Consent and Descent in American Culture.* New York: Oxford University Press, 1986.

Stember, Charles Herbert. *Sexual Racism: The Emotional Barrier to an Integrated Society.* New York: Elsevier, 1976.

Stepto, Robert B. *From Behind the Veil: A Study of Afro-American Narrative.* 2nd ed. 1979. Chicago: University of Illinois Press, 1991.

Sundquist, Eric J. *To Wake the Nations: Race in the Making of American Literature.* Cambridge: Harvard University Press, 1993.

Sutherland, Sidney. "The Mystery of the Pencil Factory." In *Ten Real Murder Mysteries—Never Solved!* New York: G. P. Putnam's Sons, 1929. Online: www.mtroyal.ab.ca/gaslight/penclfct.htm.

Theweleit, Klaus. *Male Bodies: Psychoanalyzing the White Terror.* 1978. Vol. 2 of *Male Fantasies.* Trans. Erica Carter and Chris Turner, in collaboration with Stephen Conway. Minneapolis: University of Minnesota Press, 1989.

They Won't Forget. Dir. Mervyn Leroy. 1937.

Trachtenberg, Joshua. *The Devil and the Jews: The Medieval Conception of the Jew and Its Relation to Modern Anti-Semitism.* 1943. Philadelphia: Jewish Publication Society of America, 1983.

Tumin, Melvin M. "What is Antisemitism?" In *Antisemitism in the United States.* Ed. Leonard Dinnerstein, 10–16. New York: Holt, Rinehart and Winston, 1971.

Turner, George Kibbe. "The Daughters of the Poor." *McClure's* 34.1 (Nov. 1909): 45–61.

———. "Tammany's Control of New York by Professional Criminals." *McClure's* 33.2 (June 1909): 117–34.

Twain, Mark. *The Adventures of Huckleberry Finn.* Ed. Leo Marx. Indianapolis: Bobbs-Merrill, 1969.

Wade, Wyn Craig. *The Fiery Cross: The Ku Klux Klan in America.* 1987. New York: Simon and Schuster, 1988.

Walkowitz, Judith R. "Jack the Ripper and the Myth of Male Violence." *Feminist Studies* 8.3 (Fall 1982): 543–74.

Waskow, Arthur I. *From Race Riot to Sit-In, 1919 and the 1960s: A Study in the Connections Between Conflict and Violence.* Garden City, N.Y.: Doubleday, 1966.

White, Walter. *Flight.* New York: Knopf, 1926.

———. *A Man Called White: The Autobiography of Walter White.* Bloomington: Indiana University Press, 1948.

Whitfield, Stephen J. "Jews and Other Southerners: Counterpoint and Paradox." In *"Turn to the South": Essays on Southern Jewry.* Ed. Nathan M. Kaganoff and Melvin I. Urofsky, 76–104. Charlottesville: University of Virginia Press, 1979.

Wiggins, Gene. *Fiddlin' Georgia Crazy: Fiddlin' John Carson, His Real World, and the World of His Songs.* Urbana: University of Illinois Press, 1987.

Williams, Patricia J. "On Imagining Foes, Imagining Friendship." In *Struggles in the Promised Land: Toward a History of Black-Jewish Relations in the United States.* Ed. Jack Salzman and Cornel West, 371–83. New York: Oxford University Press, 1997.

Williamson, Joel. *The Crucible of Race: Black-White Relations in the American South Since Emancipation.* New York: Oxford University Press, 1984.

Woodward, C. Vann. *Origins of the New South, 1877–1913.* 1951. Vol. 20 of *A History of the South.* Ed. Wendell Holmes Stephenson and E. Merton Coulter. Baton Rouge: Louisiana State University Press, 1987.

———. *Tom Watson: Agrarian Rebel.* 1938. New York: Oxford University Press, 1963.

Zangwill, Israel. *The Melting Pot.* 1909. New York: MacMillan, 1932.

INDEX